CONTEMPORARY
FREUD

Turning Points & Critical Issues

CONTEMPORARY FREUD
Turning Points & Critical Issues

Series Founded by Robert Wallerstein

On Freud's "Analysis Terminable and Interminable"
Edited by Joseph Sandler

On Freud's "On Narcissism: An Introduction"
Edited by Joseph Sandler, Ethel Spector Person, and
Peter Fonagy

On Freud's "Observations on Transference-Love"
Edited by Ethel Spector Person, Aiban Hagelin, and
Peter Fonagy

On Freud's "Creative Writers and Day-dreaming"
Edited by Ethel Spector Person, Peter Fonagy, and
Sérvulo Augusto Figueira

On Freud's "A Child Is Being Beaten"
Edited by Ethel Spector Person

On Freud's "Group Psychology and the Analysis of the Ego"
Edited by Ethel Spector Person

ON FREUD'S

"Group Psychology and the Analysis of the Ego"

EDITED BY ETHEL SPECTOR PERSON

FOR THE INTERNATIONAL

PSYCHOANALYTICAL ASSOCIATION

THE ANALYTIC PRESS

2001   Hillsdale, NJ   London

Published by
The Analytic Press, Inc., Publishers
Editorial Offices:
101 West Street
Hillsdale, New Jersey 07642
www.analyticpress.com

Designed by Jill Breitbarth

Set in Times & Optima by
Christopher Jaworski, Qualitext
qualitext@earthlink.net

Index by Leonard S. Rosenbaum

Library of Congress Cataloging-in-Publication Data

On Freud's "Group psychology and the analysis of the ego" /
edited by Ethel Spector Person
p.   cm. — (Contemporary Freud)
Includes bibliographical references and index.
ISBN 0-88163-325-9
1. Freud, Sigmund, 1856–1939. Massenpsychologie und Ich-Analyse.
2. Psychoanalysis. I. Person, Ethel Spector. II. Freud, Sigmund, 1856–1939.
Massenpsychologie und Ich-Analyse. English. III. International Psycho-
Analytical Association. IV. Series.

BF173.O545 2001
150.19′52—dc21
2001022680

Printed in the United States of America
10 9 8 7 6 5 4 3 2 1

Dedication

In memory of Didier Anzieu,
one of our most generative psychoanalysts,
who made a major contribution
to the way we understand group psychology

Contents

vii

Preface

The IPA Monograph Series "Contemporary Freud: Turning Points and Critical Issues" was first proposed by Robert Wallerstein as a means of fostering the exchange of psychoanalytic ideas among the several regions of the psychoanalytic world. Given the somewhat different emphases within regions and even within one region, the idea is to disseminate some unique regional perspectives, as well as the congruencies and divergences among these regions, by bringing together a number of distinguished psychoanalysts to discuss one of Freud's essays, Freud embodying our common heritage.

Each volume opens with one of Freud's classic papers or, in this volume, an excerpt from *Group Psychology* contextualized by our editor, John Kerr, followed by contributions from a panel of leading analysts, analytic teachers, and theoreticians. Each of our contributors is asked to use Freud's observations and theories to link up with issues of current interest and concern to the reviewer.

The process for selecting the Freud paper that serves as the springboard for the discussions has been amended over time. For many years, the advisory Committee to the IPA Publications Committee, composed of scores of people from around the world, was called on to supply suggestions for the subject of the Monograph. However, because of the large number of people involved, rather than solicit the large Advisory Committee for suggestions, we have, in the past several years, asked the members of the Executive Committee of the IPA Council, along with the members of the Publications Committee, to make suggestions. Their list is the one circulated to the members of the Advisory Committee asking them to rank order their preferences.

I am doubly grateful for the input of the Advisory Board members because, in addition to making the final selection of the Freud work to be discussed, they also suggest psychoanalysts from around the world who they feel might best discuss the work chosen and address its relevance to contemporary psychoanalysis.

Each volume of the Monograph series is first published in English and has been or will be translated into the other three official languages of the IPA: French, German, and Spanish. In addition, the series is published in Italy.

I have been fortunate to work for a number of years with Janice Ahmed, IPA Publications Administrator. Only through her concerted efforts, dedication, skill, and patience is it possible to manage an international publishing venture such as this. John Azelvandre, my administrative assistant, undertook responsibility for transcribing the manuscripts, updating corrections, and keeping track of deadlines with admirable attention to detail.

Much appreciation is due to Dr. Robert Tyson, the Secretary of the IPA, who has acted in every possible way to facilitate the publication of the volume, no easy task since we were in transition from one publisher to another.

This volume is the first of the Monograph Series to be published with The Analytic Press rather than with Yale University Press. We are extremely pleased to secure TAP as publisher for this series at a time when Yale University Press has reduced its commitment to psychoanalytic publishing, coinciding with the retirement of our longtime editor, Gladys Topkis.

Gladys Topkis's help was invaluable both in launching and maintaining this series. For the entire span of our relationship with Yale University Press, Gladys was our editor. Her nurturance of this series extended to facilitating the transition to The Analytic Press. She recommended us not only to The Analytic Press but also to our new editor, John Kerr.

John Kerr, in addition to being an editor, was trained as a clinical psychologist and is a contributor to the psychoanalytic literature in his own right. He is the author of the remarkably researched and brilliantly conceived book, *A Most Dangerous Method: The Story of Freud, Jung, and Sabina Spielrein*. He, like Gladys Topkis, is a great enthusiast, supporter, and friend of psychoanalysis and, like Gladys, one of the great contemporary psychoanalytic editors.

This volume presented us with a special problem. Permission to reprint from *Group Psychology* was restricted to a fixed number of pages. John Kerr made the difficult choices of which parts of *Group Psychology* to reprint (no mean feat) and contributed the text that accompanies those excerpts. His exegesis of the text stands as a major contribution to this volume.

We extend our thanks to Nancy Liguori, Lenni Kobrin, and Joan Riegel at The Analytic Press, who have provided us with careful editing, skill, and enthusiasm in bringing this volume to its conclusion. Our thanks, too, to Paul Stepansky, Managing Director of The Analytic Press, who contributes mightily to the health of contemporary psychoanalysis through his commitment to publishing psychoanalytic books and journals of merit.

This volume is dedicated to Didier Anzieu, who not too long before his death completed the chapter published in this volume. We are grateful to be able to publish it and remember Anzieu with great respect and admiration as one of the foremost contributors to psychoanalysis.

ETHEL SPECTOR PERSON

Introduction

ETHEL SPECTOR PERSON

As noted in the Preface, the policy of the IPA Publications Committee has been to select, by vote of its Advisory Board, the Freud work that will serve as the springboard for the IPA Monograph Series. Its members vote their preference among several different suggestions. In previous years, a clear majority vote coalesced with general agreement that the work chosen was of central importance to Freud's thinking and to his legacy. Not so for *Group Psychology and the Analysis of the Ego,* which elicited polarized evaluations from the members of the Advisory Board. Some of the analysts voting thought it was a major work, one that opened up new venues of investigation to psychoanalysts—for example, in its psychological exploration of the genesis of man's "thirst for obedience." Others regarded it, at best, as a sidebar to analysis or, at worst, as an inferior piece of work, particularly insofar as it reiterated Freud's much criticized thinking about the primal horde. Nonetheless, it garnered the largest number of votes, although by a small margin. Given the cogent commentaries presented herein by some of our leading analysts, I believe *Group Psychology* is an excellent choice, representing as it does a half-turn, if not a whole new turn, in Freud's thinking.

Psychoanalysts are not alone in their polarized views of this work. For example, Elias Canetti and Ernest Becker, each of whom had strong feelings about *Group Psychology,* came down on diametrically opposite sides in their evaluation of it. Canetti, a prototypical peripatetic European intellectual and perhaps one of the 20th century's most original thinkers, wrote a landmark book on social theory, *Crowds and Power* (1960), which he began working on in the 1920s in Vienna and finished 35 years later. Not only was Canetti's subject matter related to Freud's *Group Psychology,* but he was psychologically involved with Freud, as he recounts in his memoir, *A Torch in My Ear:*

At the time, I was unaware of how much the manner of my enterprise owed to the fact that there was someone like Freud in Vienna, that people talked about him in such a way as if every individual could, by himself, of his own accord, and of his own result, find explanations for things. Since Freud's ideas did not suffice for me, failing to explain the phenomenon that was most important to me, I was sincerely, if naively, convinced that I was undertaking something totally independent of him. It was clear to me that I needed him as an adversary. But the fact that he served as a kind of model for me—this was something that no one could have made me see at that time [Canetti, 1980, p. 122].

Canetti's life work was inspired by a crowd experience he witnessed in the years he spent with his mother and brother in Frankfurt (1921–1924) just before they moved to Vienna.

Early on, about one year after arriving in Frankfurt, I had watched a workers' demonstration on the *Zeil*. They were protesting the murder of Rathenau. . . . There was no end of them. I sensed a powerful conviction emanating from them; it grew more powerful. . . . The memory of this first demonstration that I consciously witnessed was powerful. It was the physical attraction that I couldn't forget [1982, pp. 79–80].

With the escalating monetary inflation, Canetti's mother and younger brothers left for Vienna, where he joined them six months later. During his first winter in Vienna (1924–1925) he had a further "illumination." This illumination, which he experienced as a revelation and calling, led him to begin his 35-year-long exploration of how power comes into being in a crowd and how it feeds back upon itself. Canetti's central insight was that the crowd instinct exists in conflict with the personality instinct. For Canetti, the struggles between those two instincts explain all of human history. (This observation echoes Freud's [1921] remark that, "while with isolated individuals personal interest is almost the only motive force, with groups it is very rarely prominent" [1921, p. 79].) Canetti concluded that the crowd instinct is as powerful as the sexual instinct.

Later, still in Vienna, he had a second crowd experience. On July 15, 1927, after workers had been killed in Burgenland and the court judged the murderers not guilty, the workers protested and Canetti became part of the crowd. "Fifty-three years have passed and the agitation of that day is still in my bones. . . . Since then, I have known quite precisely that I would not have to read a single word about the storming of the Bastille. I became a part of the crowd, I fully dissolved in it, I did not feel the slightest resistance to what the crowd was doing" (Canetti, 1980, p. 245). He described the experience as analogous to "what is known in physics as gravitation." He went to say that "the thing that happened to you in the crowd, a total alteration of consciousness, was both drastic and enigmatic. . . . The riddle wouldn't stop haunting me; it has stuck to me for the better part of my life. And if I did ultimately hit upon a few things, I was still as puzzled as ever" (p. 80).

The key experience for Canetti was that he had been

> *moved* by the crowd. . . . it was an intoxication; you were lost, you forgot yourself, you felt tremendously remote and yet fulfilled; whatever you felt, you didn't feel it for yourself; it was the most selfless thing you knew; and since selfishness was shown, talked and *threatened* on all sides, you needed this experience of thunderous unselfishness like the blast of the trumpet at the Last Judgment and you made sure not to belittle or denigrate this experience [p. 94].

It was at the farm retreat where he began his crowd study that Canetti first read Freud's *Massenpsychologie und Ich-Analyse* (as it was called in German): "I was surprised at myself for managing to open up this book out here, even though it repelled me from the very first word, and still repels me no less fifty-five years later." Manifestly, what Canetti held against Freud was that Freud lacked any personal experience of "falling prey" to the crowd: "My rejection of Freud came at the start of my work on [my] book" (p. 149).

Although Canetti acknowledged himself as tangled up with Freud as a necessary "adversary," you would never guess it from reading *Crowds and Power* (1960). Quite the contrary. In a book with a voluminous bibliography, no reference to Freud is to be found. There is but a single reference to Freud throughout, and it appears in a footnote describing Schreber's paranoid delusions, which obviously mandated some mention of Freud.

In contrast to Canetti, Ernest Becker greatly admired *Group Psychology and the Analysis of the Ego,* and it played a major role in his thinking.

In his most important work, *The Denial of Death,* Becker's (1973) comments turn to high praise:

> With a theoretical background that unlocked the problem of hypno-
> sis and that discovered the universal mechanism of the transference,
> Freud was almost obliged to provide the best insights ever into the
> psychology of leadership; and so he wrote his great work, *Group
> Psychology and the Analysis of the Ego,* a book of fewer than one
> hundred pages that in my opinion is probably the single most
> potentially liberating tract that has ever been fashioned by man [pp.
> 131–132].

Becker is less interested in the crowd per se than is Canetti. In this, he follows Freud, who was equally interested in groups and in crowds and in more organized groups with a leader.

Freud saw that people have a craving for direction and authority. For Becker, man's penchant for obedience, as evident in the attachment of group members to the leader, parallels the contemporary patient's trans-ference to a psychoanalyst or an earlier patient's submission to a hypnotist. Here Becker follows Freud so closely that, in outlining his own position on the psychology of blind obedience, he resorts freely to quoting and paraphrasing him:

> It is not so much that man is a herd animal . . . said Freud, but that
> he is a horde animal led by a chief. It is this alone that can explain
> the "uncanny and coercive characteristics of group formations."
> The chief is a "dangerous personality, toward whom only a passive-
> masochistic attitude is possible, to whom one's will has to be
> surrendered—while to be alone with him . . . appears a hazardous
> enterprise." This alone, says Freud, explains the "paralysis" that
> exists in the link between a person with inferior power to one of
> superior power. Man has "an extreme passion for authority" and
> "wishes to be governed by unrestricted force." It is this trait that the
> leader hypnotically embodies in his masterful person. . . . And so,
> as Freud argues, it is not that groups bring out anything new in
> people; it is just that they satisfy the deep-seated erotic longings that
> people constantly carry around unconsciously. For Freud, this was
> the life force that held groups together. It functioned as a kind of

psychic cement that locked people into mutual and mindless inter-
dependence: the magnetic powers of the leader, reciprocated by the
guilty delegation of everyone's will to him [pp. 131–133].

Freud (1921) believed that what Le Bon (1825) called "our thirst for
obedience" should be interpreted libidinally. He bolstered his claim that
the group bond is essentially erotic by analogizing it to love and hypnosis.
He suggested that love is the core of the group mind. He went so far as to
assert that "[h]ypnosis has a good claim to be described as a group of two"
(p. 127). Yet this is necessarily a flawed analogy. As José Brunner (1995)
points out, "Only the hypnotized person corresponds to the group members, while the hypnotist represents the leader standing above it—thus,
the hypnotic relationship contains a crowd of one" (p. 177).

Despite Becker's great admiration for *Group Psychology,* he proposed
different dynamics to explain man's thirst for obedience. For Becker, the
delegation of will to the leader is guilty (Freud's term) not because it is
erotic, but because it is propelled by weakness and constitutes abdication
of one's own agency. I believe that Becker (1973) may have come close
to the mark in explaining blind obedience when he suggested that man is

not just a naturally and lustfully destructive animal that lays waste
around him because he feels omnipotent and impregnable. Rather,
he is a trembling animal who pulls the world down around his
shoulders as he clutches for protection and support and tries to
affirm in a cowardly way his feeble powers. The qualities of the
leader, then, and the problems of people fit together in a natural
symbiosis [p. 139].

Freud never entirely disentangled the role of libido from the role of
powerlessness in the genesis of transference in its larger, nonclinical sense.
In *Group Psychology,* he fundamentally still adheres to an instinctual
framework. His growing recognition of the individual's awareness of his
powerlessness as a motive force in development is only embryonic, but it
will become visible, if not preeminent, in his work of the next few years.
He still falls short of acknowledging how much group psychology depends
on our longing for a reincarnation of the protection afforded by the parents
of early life, or sometimes on our attraction to a charismatic figure who
legitimizes the expression of our destructive urges. However, as Becker

demonstrates, Freud's notion of "transference," in its larger meaning, changed over time, moving from his belief that it was exclusively erotic in origin to a broader construction of its genesis in his later work, for example, in *The Future of an Illusion*, in which he speaks of the issues of "human weakness" and "childish helplessness" and begins to address our longing for a powerful father as a "protection against strange superior powers" (Freud, 1928, p. 24).

In "*Group Psychology and the Analysis of the Ego:* The Text," John Kerr interweaves excerpts from *Group Psychology* with an exegesis that contextualizes it. Ironically, it turned out that we were fortunate in being restricted as to how much of the text we could reprint; otherwise we would have lost Kerr's brilliantly virtuoso close reading of the text. Both clinical psychologist and psychoanalytic historian, Kerr distinguishes for us the difference in the ways the historian of ideas and the psychoanalyst look at texts. But regarding this particular text, Kerr concludes that the historian of ideas must come up short, given the paucity of material that might be considered primary source material. Therefore "one is invited, even forced, to read more like a clinician after all, that is, identifying onself with the concerns of the text, though this need not mean sacrificing one's critical distance." For Kerr, "the subtext [is] that there is something very important being said here but that it is up to the reader to finish the argument for himself or herself."

Kerr points out how Freud takes contagion and gregariousness as they appear in the work of Trotter and McDougall and libidinizes them and how he takes Le Bon's influence of the leader and oedipalizes it. But Kerr also observes that there are "two huge and unexpected wrinkles in [Freud's] argument." Libido is not the ordinary kind but is aim inhibited. Kerr's exegesis is a nuanced consideration of the way Freud here uses the notions of aim-inhibited libido, the ego ideal, being "in love" and idealization to explicate Freud's extremely subtle arguments. Kerr underscores Freud's conclusion that "a primary group . . . is a number of individuals who have put one and the same object in the place of their ego ideal and consequently identify themselves with one another in their ego." Similarly, the father in Freud's argument is shown not to be the typical oedipal father of childhood, but a revenant of the father of the primal hoard. I cannot do justice to Kerr's analysis of the text in a summary, except to say that it is a remarkable demonstration of what can result once one masters the art of close reading.

Our distinguished contributors track the relevance of *Group Psychology and the Analysis of the Ego* to our current thinking, not omitting to comment on what now seems questionable or outdated. Didier Anzieu presents the historical background against which *Group Psychology* was written. He proceeds to give an excellent summary of its sequential sections, serendipitously so for our project because, by virtue of the copyright strictures already alluded to in the Preface, we were unable to reprint the entire text. Anzieu notes that, following the composition of the metapsychological texts of 1915, Freud "in the years 1920–1923, . . . published the three fundamental writings in which he corrected his earlier views and advanced beyond them." He means, of course, *Beyond the Pleasure Principle* (1920), *Group Psychology and the Analysis of the Ego* (1921), and *The Ego and the Id* (1923).

With regard to the text at hand, Anzieu raises the intriguing possibility that group dynamics within psychoanalytic societies and the International Psychoanalytical Association might have been a stimulus to Freud's reflections on group psychology. He traces the development of psychoanalytic thinking on group process in the work of Wilfred Bion, S. H. Foulkes, John Rickman at London's Tavistock Clinic, and André Ruffiot. And finally Anzieu discusses his own work, in which he postulates analogies between groups and dreams.

Robert Caper affirms the importance of *Group Psychology* from a different perspective altogether, noting that

> individual human psychology cannot be isolated from group psychology, not simply because one of the functions of the mind is to form relationships with objects, but because the individual's relationship to the object is an integral part of the mind itself. A mind without links to objects is simply not a human mind, and one simply cannot, therefore, have an adequate picture of the individual human mind without considering the links that the mind has to its objects.

Caper remarks that Freud approached this link through a concept he had only recently developed, that in the boy's relationship to his father there were two kinds of identification, an omnipotent identification in which he believes he *is* the father and an aspiration *to be like* the father while preserving the father as a distinct object. Caper analogizes this distinction to the difference between unorganized groups and organized groups, unorganized groups being like the mob, in which the individual loses his sense of distinctness, while organized groups allow a member to keep his own identity. These, in turn, can be related to Bion's (1961) primitive and sophisticated groups. The former, Bion's basic assumption group, corresponds to Freud's unorganized group, while the work group corresponds to Freud's organized group. In his interesting and original contribution, Caper argues that the psychoanalytic dyad might itself be regarded as a group of two, which combines elements of both primitive and sophisticated psychoanalytic groups. (Because Caper is not postulating an authoritarian analyst, his analogy of the psychoanalytic dyad as a group of two is more compelling than the analogy of the hypnotist and his subject as a group of two.)

Abraham Zaleznik likewise sees groups as consisting of two kinds: primary groups and artificial groups or larger organizations, which Zaleznik prefers to refer to as "complex organizations." We are fortunate to have a psychoanalyst who is a major organizational consultant available to explore this latter kind of organization, which includes those ever more dominant institutions, large modern corporations. (Zaleznik's consideration of the corporation parallels what Caper would refer to as a working group.)

The corporation must appeal to the members' interests, what Zaleznik calls "interest politics." His chapter details the influence of the leader on the led in modern corporations "where, at first glance, neither libido nor identification would seem to account for group formations and behavior." Instead, he suggests, one must look at the role of self-interest: this is extremely important, as Zaleznik clearly disengages from an exclusive emphasis on oedipal dynamics. However, he explores an important distinction in the dynamics between corporations, based on self-interest and family businesses in which passions often supersede self-interest, another demonstration of two different kinds of groups.

If Zaleznik is primarily discussing what Caper calls "work groups," then André Haynal is addressing basic assumption groups. Coexisting alongside apparently rationally run corporations are those many fanatical groups that have distorted recent history. Haynal gives a clarion call to take seriously the history of fanaticism, including its frequent connection to religious beliefs and to secular doctrines as well. While Zaleznik, who focuses on corporations, does not observe the passionate submission to the leader that Freud described in *Group Psychology*," Haynal describes "the quasi-hypnotic submission to [the leader's] voice and the projection of all our hopes and ideals on him." Haynal closes with a heartfelt alarum, also voiced by Eizirik and in a different way by Anzieu, to the effect that psychoanalysis itself may have aspects of religion in which there are impulses to expel those who defy its basic principles.

In addition to his own contribution, Haynal secured the permission to reprint Ernst Falzeder's "family trees" of psychoanalytic "schools," which is a marvelous contribution in its own right.

Yolanda Gampel puts Freud's ideas about group psychology and mobs within the context of millennial culture, in which "globalized capital creates a new transnational class of the weak linked by satellites." Given the global consumer culture, she observes a confusion between mass psychology and individual psychology. She writes that "the history of our time lies somewhere between the image of historical religious myth . . . and the image brought by the media, which preserves, almost automatically, the myth of modern life." Western culture "generally [accepts the] claim that racism is the collective parallel to individual narcissism, a nonacceptance of the difference of the other, and a rejection of the similarities between the in-group and the other." Like Caper, she draws on Bion's seminal ideas. What Freud called drives, Bion saw as assuming a "double-aspect in man . . . the rational-scientific and the irrational-primitive lost in fantasy." Gampel describes her clinical experience treating patients who went through extreme situations of social violence and shares with us excerpts from personal testimony generated in group therapy. To understand the plight of these patients, she draws on the concept of "radioactivity," an external reality that enters the psyche and over which the individual has no control.

Cláudio Eizirik, like Anzieu, summarizes the different sections of *Group Psychology and the Analysis of the Ego,* though with less emphasis on its metapsychological architecture. He points out that, while the ego and the drives are explored at some length in *Group Psychology,* the paper is primarily a contribution to understanding social processes, and it is along this arc that Eizirik's exegesis proceeds. He traces a line of development from *Group Psychology* to Wilfred Bion, Elliot Jaques, Janine Chasseguet-Smirgel, and Otto Kernberg. From there he considers anew the current relationship between psychoanalysis and culture, in an effort to determine whether they are friends or foes—or something in between. And, finally, he proposes to address, indeed confront, the psychoanalytic movement itself as an artificially structured group, all too much like the Church hierarchy or the Army as described by Freud. He describes what he hopes will be a method to counteract the dissension and splintering within the psychoanalytic movement that has taken place since the death of Freud. To counter the illusory power of psychoanalysis, Eizirik proposes "verification theories, outcome studies, and a permanent dialogue with other disciplines." My brief summary cannot do justice to Eizirik's complex consideration of the past illusions to which some psychoanalysts still adhere.

For all Freud's reluctance to abandon instinctual life and oedipal dynamics as the almost exclusive motivating forces in our lives, in *Group Psychology* he begins to emphasize the importance of the experience of interpersonal life as decisive in shaping inner life: "In the individual's mental life, someone else is invariably involved, as a model, as an object, as a helper, as an opponent; and so from the very first individual psychology, in this extended but entirely justifiable sense of the words is at the same time social psychology as well" (Freud, 1921, p. 69).

Freud also suggests further areas for investigation based on his observation of the nature of relationships:

> The evidence of psycho-analysis shows that almost every intimate emotional relation between two people which lasts for some time— marriage, friendship, the relations between parents and children— contains a sediment of feelings of aversion and hostility, which only escapes perception as a result of repression. This is less disguised in the common wrangles between business partners or in the grumbles of a subordinate at his superior. . . . In the undisguised antipathies and aversions which people feel toward strangers with whom they have to do, we may recognize the expression of self-love—narcissism [pp. 101–102].

In the last passage, it seems to me that Freud may be addressing, among other negative feelings, the role that reaction formation against envy plays in our lives. Overall, Freud here introduces a whole new perspective on the primary role of affect (as distinct from drive) in human motivation, one that is fully explicated only in more recent psychoanalytic investigations.

A broadened view of the essential components of the individual's psyche, as essentially linked to life with others yet capable of standing independently, is mirrored by the paradox of Freud's own authorial stance throughout the text. As early as the third chapter of *Group Psychology,* we find Freud inserting a curious statement about his standing alone: "as regarding intellectual work, it remains a fact, indeed, that great decisions in the realm of thought and momentous discoveries and solutions of problems are only possible to an individual working in solitude" (p. 83). Here he expresses a heroic view typical of the 19th and early 20th centuries. Set this comment in juxtaposition to Canetti's (1980) own bias, previously quoted:

> At the time, I was unaware of how much the manner of my enterprise owed to the fact that there was someone like Freud in Vienna, that people talked about him in such a way as if every individual could, by himself, of his own accord, and of his own resolve, find explanations for things. Since Freud's ideas did not suffice for me, failing to explain the phenomenon that was most important to me, I was sincerely, if not naively, convinced that I was undertaking something totally independent of him [p. 122].

Both shared the wishful fantasy of the independent genius who stands above the crowd.

Contrast that with how scientists now so often regard each other as integral parts of a team, and how proud they are of the "labs" with which they are affiliated. While they recognize a hierarchy among themselves, they acknowledge their involvement in a group endeavor. How paradoxical it is that Canetti and Freud, both dedicated to understanding the essential role of group psychology in the formation of the individual psyche, nonetheless are committed to their belief in the individual's striving for genius in isolation. Given that it was the belief system of their time that achievement was individual, this was a position Freud could adhere to despite the fact that he used a series of transference objects or "creative collaborators" of greater or lesser gifts in the furtherance of his own work—for example, Wilhelm Fliess (Person, 1999).

The current psychoanalytic interest in and emphasis on self–object relations and intersubjectivity is the outgrowth of an internal dynamic within the evolution of our field, but it reflects, too, a more widespread cultural skepticism about great men and great leaders and a much greater appreciation of the way each of us is culturally embedded, not just within a group but within a particular historical sensibility (Person, 1995, pp. 197–217). Ironically, it was Freud, one of our last great self-proclaimed individualists (individualist manqué, perhaps), who, with some others, paved the way to our understanding ourselves within the context of the group. Nowadays our study of groups and group formation is enhanced through the insights generated within theories of object relations and intersubjectivity and also from a greater appreciation of the impact of the historical moment. None of us, not even Freud, is free of the cultural unconscious, the myths that permeate our thinking.

REFERENCES

Becker, E. (1973), *The Denial of Death*. New York: Free Press.

Bion, W. R. (1961), *Experiences in Groups*. London: Tavistock.

Brunner, J. (1995), *Freud and the Politics of Psychoanalysis*. Oxford: Blackwell.

Canetti, E. (1960), *Crowds and Power* [*Masse und Macht*]. New York: Continuum, 1972.

Canetti, E. (1980), *The Torch in My Ear*. Farrar, Straus, & Giroux, 1982.

Freud, S. (1920), *Beyond the Pleasure Principle. Standard Edition,* 18: 7–64. London: Hogarth Press, 1955.

Freud, S. (1921), *Group Psychology and the Analysis of the Ego. Standard Edition,* 18:69–143. London: Hogarth Press, 1955.

Freud, S. (1923), *The Ego and the Id. Standard Edition,* 19:12–66. London: Hogarth Press, 1961.

Freud, S. (1928), *The Future of an Illusion. Standard Edition,* 21:1–56. London: Hogarth Press, 1961.

Le Bon, G. (1895), *La Psychologie des Foules*. Paris: Felix Alcan.

Person, E. (1995), *By Force of Fantasy*. New York: Basic Books.

Person, E. (1999), Creative collaborations: Writers and editors. *The Psychoanalytic Study of the Child,* 54:1–16. New Haven, CT: Yale University Press.

PART ONE

Group Psychology and the Analysis of the Ego (1921)
The Text

JOHN KERR

Group Psychology and the Analysis of the Ego (1921)
The Text

JOHN KERR

This is not an easy text to begin, it is not an easy text to read, and it is not an easy text to be done with.

I

It is not an easy text to begin.

A clinician typically begins a text by assuming, a bit boldly but also out of epistemic necessity, that clinical experiences are more or less timeless. In a sense, the clinician reads looking to find and refind the present. This orientation toward the present carries over into how he or she begins. The clinician tries to find a common point of reference, either in the concepts being used or in the descriptions of patients, or in both, with a view to sharing in what is being said. Disagreement is allowed, in principle, but sharing is how one starts. Identification on some level is the price of admission. It is also the basis for intellectual profit.

But *Group Psychology and the Analysis of the Ego* is not a clinical text. There are no patients in it. And its concepts, as we shall see, are less accessible to today's clinicians than might be supposed.

The historian of ideas begins quite differently. The text is external, and the historian means to keep it that way. The orientation is toward the past. Processes of empathy do come into play but only insofar as they must to keep matters humanly comprehensible. Otherwise, one begins in an

3

altogether cautious spirit. One tries to date the inception from primary materials, identify the precipitating inspiration, and then, so far as this is possible, chart the inevitable influences and prior experiences leading up to both. For the historian, the proper way to begin a text is by standing back, not jumping in.

In the case of Freud's (1921) *Group Psychology and the Analysis of the Ego,* this kind of analysis cannot be adequately made. For some idea of just how hard it might be to try, let us consider the only published piece of primary source material we have bearing on the text's inception and inspiration.

On May 12, 1919, Freud wrote Sándor Ferenczi, saying that, on receiving news recently from "Toni" (their mutual friend, patron, and patient, the terminally ill Anton von Freund), "an inhibition in my up to then increased productivity set in." Now tumbles out the mention of the text's inception: "I had not only completed the draft of 'Beyond the Pleasure Principle,' which is being copied out for you, but I also took up the little thing about the 'uncanny' again, and, with a simple-minded idea [*Einfall*], I attempted a Psy-A foundation for group psychology. Now that should rest" (Falzeder and Brabant, 1996, p. 354).

Historical paydirt? Dust, really. Putting the information in context, we can place Freud's start within a two- to three-week period. Nice. But we are in the dark as to what precisely he was thinking. He is explicit: a chance thought, unbidden, came to mind—literally an *Einfall,* translated in his clinical works as "free association." It could have come from anywhere and been about anything.

Nor does the documentary record get any better subsequently. From a letter to Abraham a year later, we know that Freud turned his "idea" into a "paper" and planned during the summer of 1920 to turn that into a "small book," which he did (Abraham and Freud, 1965, p. 308). Members of the secret Committee received their copies the following summer, shortly before the week-long rendezvous of the ensemble in the Harz Mountains began on September 21, 1921. One can also deduce from the extant published correspondence that Karl Abraham and Ernest Jones were familiar with it prior to publication, from the text itself that Otto Rank was as well, and it is a very safe bet that Ferenczi had seen it, too. Which may partly explain why there was so little discussion of it after it came out. But none of this information throws any further light on its genesis, nor on any influences prior to it.

There is virtually nothing to go on, save what can be found in the text itself. One is entitled in this situation to follow Freud's lead and see what topics come up and how the argument goes. One is invited, even forced, to read more like a clinician after all, that is, identifying oneself with the concerns of the text, though this need not mean sacrificing one's critical distance. What one discovers this way, to be sure, falls well short of historical understanding. One can hope to illumine the text, not explain it. But this is worth doing if done well. Moreover, the exercise draws one toward a vastly important topic. Indeed, it is principally in its ability to provoke just such attempts at illumination and further reflection that the text has greatest value for today's reader.

In the description and partial abridgment of *Group Psychology and the Analysis of the Ego* that follows, the subtext is that there is something very important being said here but that it is up to the reader to finish the argument for himself or herself.

II

It is not an easy text to read.

To begin with, some readers bring their own initial misapprehension to the text. Once the reader hears that the group is "impulsive, changeable and irritable" and also "generous or cruel, heroic or cowardly" (Freud, 1921, p. 77), that it "is extraordinarily credulous and open to influence," that it "goes directly to extremes" (p. 78), and that it "wants to be ruled and oppressed and to fear its masters" (pp. 77–78), the reader assumes, not unreasonably, that we are dealing here with the irrational side of group psychology. The reader may assume further that this irrational side stands in some easy-to-understand relation to the irrational side of the individual.

Readers who start this way, and many do, are off on the wrong foot. For Freud is not saying that the irrational is a side of group psychology; for Freud, it is the whole of it. As to any connection with individual irrationality, especially as found in neurosis, it will take the entire book to clear that up. Given this kind of opening misapprehension on the reader's part, Freud has extra work to do. It will behoove him to be extra clear.

For long stretches, indeed for more than 4/5ths of the book, the style *is* clear, Freud writing with his customary expository ease. And here let *us* be clear: When Freud is in his stride, his prose is a pleasure. He generates a back-and-forth rhythm that he can take forward and deeper into the argument, or sideways as he pauses for second and third thoughts, or even backward as he returns to an issue, usually noted at the time, that he has left hanging. Point–counterpoint, thesis–rejoinder, agreement–reservation, boldness–caution, certainty–doubt–certainty. It has become fashionable nowadays to buffet James Strachey about the poor translator's head and ears for things like rendering the German "*Ich*" as "ego" instead of "I"—this mortal sin appears in the very title of the present work—but he has taken an accomplished German stylist and given us an accomplished English one. Occasionally, we should let ourselves be grateful.

The expository touch comes through in Strachey's rendering. Freud seems always to be musing out loud, contemplating and considering, never merely describing or arguing. This takes more time than a straightforward approach might, but the effect is not labored; it is consistently agreeable. Consider the following, which comes very, very early in the text as Freud tries to establish in chapter one that his version of "I-psychology" may be relevant to "group psychology." Freud has already conceded at the outset that a good portion of individual psychology involves relations with others; if this concession in an interpersonal or relational direction costs him anything, as some modern readers might suppose, he does not show it. Instead, he advances toward his first goal, which is nothing less than his right to speak, while seeming merely to take stock of the situation:

> The individual in the relations which have already been mentioned—to his parents and to his bothers and sisters, to the person he is in love with, to his friend, and to his physician—comes under the influence of only a single person, or of a very small number of persons, each of whom has become enormously important to him. Now in speaking of social or group psychology it has become usual to leave these relations on one side and to isolate as the subject of inquiry the influencing of an individual by a large number of people simultaneously, people with whom he is connected by something, though otherwise they may in many respects be strangers to him. Group psychology is therefore concerned with the individual man as a member of a race, or a nation, of a caste, of a profession, of an institution, or as a component part of a crowd of people who have been organized into a group at some particular time for some definite purpose.

So far, Freud seems just to be taking in the territory. Transparently, he wishes to connect the two domains, the small and intimate with the large and ascriptive; but rather than do so actively at this point, his next sentence puts the burden on those who keep them analytically divided. He remains on the sidelines a bit longer, and when he enters the fray, it is almost diffidently. The text continues:

> When once natural continuity has been severed in this way, if a breach is thus made between things which are by nature interconnected, it is easy to regard the phenomena that appear under these special conditions as being expressions of a special instinct that is not further reducible—the social instinct ("herd instinct," "group mind"), which does not come to light in any other situations. But we may perhaps venture to object that it seems difficult to attribute to the factor of number a significance so great as to make it capable by itself of arousing in our mental life a new instinct that is otherwise not brought into play. Our expectation is therefore directed toward two other possibilities: that the social instinct may not be a primitive one and insusceptible of dissection, and that it may be possible to discover the beginnings of its development in a narrower circle, such as that of the family [p. 70].

There is a lot going on in those sentences, if you look at them carefully. But nothing to disagree with, not yet at any rate. The tone is altogether companionable.

Yet this is still not an easy text to read. There is a kind of resistance, a distrust, that begins to tug at the reader's sleeve. The problem starts early in chapter two, when Freud takes up Gustav Le Bon's 1895 classic, *Psychology of Crowds,* and continues on for a good while. Freud lets Le Bon have his say all right, but he also keeps interrupting—as he freely admits. Some of the interruptions are for the purpose of disagreeing, more precisely for entering a mental reservation out loud: Le Bon fails to consider what it is in an individual that enables him to unite to the group. Le Bon sees new characteristics in the individual's behavior in the group where we see old ones freed from repression. Le Bon distinguishes two features, contagion and suggestibility, where further reflection would derive the former from the latter. Yet, at other times, Freud interrupts to agree. And sometimes, he interrupts to do both:

I have quoted this passage so fully in order to make it quite clear that Le Bon explains the condition of an individual in a group as being actually hypnotic, and does not merely make a comparison between the two states. We have no intention of raising any objection at this point, but wish only to emphasize the fact that the two last causes of an individual becoming altered in a group (the contagion and the heightened suggestibility) are evidently not on a par, since the contagion seems actually to be a manifestation of the suggestibility [p. 76].

For the most part, Freud is at pains to agree with Le Bon on the major points. The interruptions thus often say virtually the same things in Freud's own words: in the group the conscious rationality of the individual is lost and hitherto unconscious impulses rule; there is a kind of emotional contagion between group members; suggestibility runs riot; there is a strong need for and responsiveness to a leader. Freud's passages on such topics are sufficiently harmonious with the Frenchman's that when next he hands the turn back to his Gallic interlocutor, the transition is sometimes so seamless that one has to check who is speaking.

Freud's sign-off on Le Bon, a one-sentence paragraph ending chapter two, combines both ingredients: a reservation coupled with agreement expressed as pure praise: "Le Bon does not give the impression of having succeeded in bringing the function of the leader and the importance of prestige completely into harmony with his brilliantly executed picture of the group mind" (p. 81).

William McDougall's 1920 psychological text, *The Group Mind,* is not excerpted. Otherwise, in chapter three it gets much the same treatment: paraphrase at considerable length, agreement in the main, obliquely expressed reservations noted on certain points. As McDougall's text takes up "unorganized" groups, as well as staider "organized" groups, we now have three voices—his, Le Bon's, and Freud's—raising the hue and cry on the oddities of crowd behavior. Eventually, Trotter's 1916 best-seller, *Instincts of the Herd in Peace and War,* will be culled to provide a fourth voice. But consideration of Trotter is reserved for late in the book, by which time a goodly number of issues that were important early in the game already have been disposed of. Freud's need for him will be much more particular. Still, the same use is made: wonderful book, find a lot to agree with, not quite our kind.

Then there is another kind of interruption, Freud just being Freud. Sometimes he has a thought that is just too well formed to wait:

> In order to make a correct judgment upon the morals of groups, one must take into consideration the fact that when individuals come together in a group all their individual inhibitions fall away and all the cruel, brutal and destructive instincts, which lie dormant in individuals as relics of a primitive epoch, are stirred up to find free gratification. But under the influence of suggestion groups are also capable of high achievement in the shape of abnegation, unselfishness, and devotion to an ideal. While with isolated individuals personal interest is almost the only motive force, with groups it is very rarely prominent. It is possible to speak of an individual having his moral standards raised by a group [here a citation of Le Bon]. Whereas the intellectual capacity of a group is always far below that of an individual, its ethical conduct may rise as high above his as it may sink deep below it [p. 79].

In general, if Freud finds something interesting to say, he finds more than one way to say it. In particular, the topic of the individual as compared with the group member generates any number of arresting passages in the text. I shall leave these to other contributors to the present volume, who have the time to do them justice. The point just quoted, meanwhile, is a good example of a facet of Freud's expository style. As a point, it fits in well with the deep structure of Freud's argument, though that has not yet been revealed. Then, too, Freud means to get around to the Church and the Army as his two great exemplars of group behavior, so it behooves him to anticipate any reader who might accuse him of underrating the reality of either piety or valor. But Church and Army have not been brought up yet. Thus, in context, Freud seems to be simply honest, observing things as they are, even though the drift of the observation goes against what has heretofore been said about primitivity and impulsiveness in crowd behavior. It is also, we should note, generous as well as honest for Freud to cite Le Bon on the same point.

It is all honest and generous on Freud's part, and seemingly clear each step along the way. Yet the scrupulous use of sources nonetheless makes for a distracted read, in part because it simply is not possible to keep track of all the duly noted reservations amidst the general clamor of agreement.

Then, too, some of the time, one has all one can do simply to keep track of who is saying what.

The feeling of distraction is compounded by what is usually one of the more agreeable features of Freud's style. We are accustomed to Freud's speaking in more than one voice, in the service of more than one point of view, as he expresses objections or raises alternatives or whatever, as he slides in and out of his discussions with himself and also with the reader. However, the services ordinarily rendered by these other imagined voices here are provided by real voices, with names and texts and footnotes and all the other accoutrements of being real. This doesn't feel right. These other authorities just cannot be imagined on command and then evaporated without consequence when the argument turns a corner. Their recalcitrant reality ends up interpenetrating with the usual fictive personas of Freud expository voice. Freud's genial, multivocal self seems to be both dispersed and concretized at the same time as parts of it are reassigned to these other members of the circle. Or is it the other way around, with members of the circle taking up residence inside Freud's own narrative ego?

Ultimately, a reader who is trying to keep track of who is saying what, and yet also remember the noted reservations, finds his or her attention wandering and weakening. One gets distracted. In resolute counterresponse, one may well start to concentrate harder and harder, as if to say, wait a minute, I am going to get a hold on this argument, not be lulled by it. The impulse to make a chapter outline becomes quite strong—if only to stop the argument from undulating unnecessarily. In fact, two of the contributors to this volume have done exactly that, and, while I cannot speak for their motives, I can vouch that I certainly made my own chapter outline, plus a makeshift concordance between Freud and his three companions and their respective terminologies, for the reasons just given.

Underlying it all is a far bigger problem, which occurs only in English, the problem of the word "group." This is how Strachey translated Freud's word *Masse*. Thus, while the duet between Freud and Le Bon readily brings to mind "crowds" and "mobs" and "gangs," the text insists on speaking only of "group" psychology. It makes the reader decidedly uneasy. A "group" can be many things, from General Motors to a Little League team to the education committee of a psychoanalytic institute to a lynch mob. Are we talking about all of them? It seems not. To be sure, if a fellow wants to make the case that an education committee at a psychoanalytic institute can indeed behave like a lynch mob, let him. But, in that case, realism demands that we also observe that the education committee manifestly goes about its work much more slowly than the mob, slowly enough that the victim often has time to escape, even time enough to start a new institute of his or her own. That's an important difference. And we have not yet gotten to Little League teams or General Motors. Well, then, perhaps we are talking about only some aspects of group life, some shared tendencies that remain latent or checked for the most part, becoming overt only in certain circumstances or at certain times. Not the whole of group psychology is up for discussion, only some sides of it. Or perhaps we are talking about just some kinds of groups. The reader can imagine it either way.

How "group" should be construed is never made clear. It did not need to be made clear in German, since *Masse,* plural *Massen,* as in the psychology of the masses, has just the built-in lexical reach and resonance that Freud wants. But in English, not making the scope of the argument clear means standing on the soft, mushy ground of the more neutral and all-inclusive word "group." As a result, one enters the argument and takes one's seat with a mental reservation, an abiding sense of unease that will not go away. One comes quickly to understand the pews, for they are labeled: contagion, impulsive, suggestible, prestige of the leader, herd instinct, primitive, childlike, irrational, and so on and so forth. But, excuse me, which church is this?

A trip to the dictionary stand makes it clear how unsatisfactory the whole business is. If one opens the *Duden,* the equivalent of *Webster's* in the German language, as Peter Rudnytsky (personal communication) has done on my behalf, and looks up *Masse,* one finds, first of all, the idea of unformed dough, of gooey, shapeless, pasty, puffy matter. Then comes the idea of a great, though unspecified number; a "lot" one could say, as in an odd lot, but also a lot of money. The idea of a great number also turns up in the idea of mass produced, the same in German as it does in English. In politics, a *Masse* is something more than a majority; it is a preponderance; "the great mass" of voters, we might say. In Marxism, of course, it is the oppressed parts of society, the masses or *Massen.* There is the connotation of a lack of independent thought or action in these lattermost usages as well as of numbers and formlessness. There is also the word's use as a term in physics, which English shares, and, oddly enough, in German only, in matters of inheritance, where both the assets of the estate and also the physiological inheritance of the line can be rendered with the help of this word *Masse.* (The last usage has its own reverberation in the phylogenetic dimension of Freud's argument, as we shall see.)

If one also checks one's *Langenscheidt,* the premier German–English, English–German bilingual dictionary (again I have to thank Peter Rudnytsky), one finds some further idioms of interest. The *breiten Massen,* literally broad masses, is the rank and file in any group. Crowds arrive in *Massen* in German just as they arrive *en masse* in English and in French. But to go "with the crowd" in German is to go with the mass—*mit der Masse*—and a "stampede" is a *Massenflucht.* Interesting nuances; there's more than a bit of "crowd" in this word. Not to mention a sense of undifferentiation—gooey, unformed lumps. All and all, a dandy word for Freud to have available.

But it is not "group." If you check the *Langenscheidt* entry for *Masse,* the English word group does not appear. And, conversely, if you look up "group" in *Langenscheidt,* you will nowhere find *Masse.* You will find things like *Gruppe* for "group," *Kreis* for "circle," and *Konzern* for "commercial outfit"—but no *Masse.*

Hang Strachey? Not so fast. It turns out that Strachey was Freud's personal choice as translator (Paskauskas, 1993, p. 419). Indeed, as it happens, this was the first major work Strachey took on. Strachey was living in Vienna at the time he started (he was seeing Freud in analysis), and proximity figured in Freud's choice: "he is near me and I can collaborate with him" (p. 419). Moreover, Freud subsequently went over the first half of the translation before it went to press (p. 431). This half, Freud pronounced "absolutely correct, free of all misunderstandings" (p. 431). Jones agreed, calling the translation "excellently done" (p. 439).

So the choice of words that I have been complaining about, Freud was complicit in. (We ought to remember this the next time the subject of "ego" for "*Ich*" comes up.) To be sure, in English "mass" and "masses," and "mass" as an adjective, will eventually lead to some infelicities and a general lack of sonorousness in an argument so intricately inlaid as Freud's. A whiff of this awkwardness can be found in the Jones correspondence, where "Mass-Psychology" with a hyphen looks odd on the page and can sound odd when read aloud. Maybe author and translator smelled this coming. "Group," though palpably worse lexically, sounds better in many of the constructions it is needed in. Beyond this, however, the matter is inexplicable. (More unreasonably still, Strachey, by his own admission, took "crowd," a quite correct way of rendering Le Bon's "*foule*," and changed this perfectly good English word to "group" in the excerpts taken from an already published English translation of the Frenchman's work so as to harmonize. For shame.)

Yet I would be wrong to exaggerate the difficulty, real enough though it may be, and leave the reader with the very false impression that the text is unreadable. It is readable, at times as readable as can be. It just undulates somehow and also leaves one worried about what precisely we are talking about. To be sure, the latter problem improves for a time as assistance comes to author and translator from an unlikely quarter. McDougall (1920) helps out. His distinction between "organized" groups and "unorganized" groups, which first appears in chapter three, at least puts into words the tension that is mounting in the reader. More, Freud then makes it reasonably clear that McDougall's "unorganized" groups is what he has chiefly been talking about thus far, which cuts the semantic playing field down to a reasonable size. In the bargain, Freud (1921) comes out with a nifty cybernetic point all his own on how to distinguish the two kinds of groups:

> It seems to us that the condition which McDougall designates as the "organization" of a group can with more justification be described in another way. The problem consists in how to procure for the group precisely those features which were characteristic of the individual and which are extinguished in him by the formation of the group. For the individual, outside the primitive group, possessed his own continuity, his self-consciousness, his traditions and customs, his own particular functions and position, and he kept apart from his rivals. Owing to his entry into an "unorganized" group he had lost this distinctiveness for a time. . . . [w]e thus recognize that the aim is to equip the group with the attributes of the individual [pp. 86–87].

Matters would be almost crystal clear if hereafter "unorganized group" were used consistently rather than just "group," but it is not. Moreover, the compass of the argument eventually expands again to take into account two "groups," Church and Army, that are quite large and organized, unwieldy though their affairs may otherwise be. Author and translator are manifestly intent on somehow retaining all the savory connotations of

Masse full to the brim. So they continue to drink their cup of chicory, "group." Also, perhaps, being too closely in alignment with McDougall in his terminology would spoil another point, about panic, down the road—a telling point it is, too—but we will get to that shortly.

III

So where is Freud going? He has put us on alert that we are not staying where we are, that the extant accounts of the irrationality of group behavior, while commendable, will not quite do. Yet the suspense, notwithstanding his efforts to create it, is less than gripping. Freud happened a long time ago; we have a pretty good idea of how this is going to turn out. He will take the tendency to form a group tie—gregariousness in Trotter's (1920) terms, a susceptibility to contagion in McDougall's (1920), both contagion and suggestibility in Le Bon's (1895)—and he is going to libidinize it, that is, derive it according to the precepts of libido theory. And he is going to take the influence of the leader, which Le Bon's text speaks of in terms of prestige, and he is going to oedipalize it.

He does, of course. With regard to the first transformation, he announces his plan forthwith, after recapitulating some of his dissatisfactions with the formulations of Le Bon and McDougall and with the general tendency to rely too squarely on "suggestion" as a catchall explanation. Freud's (1921) plan gets its own succinct paragraph: "Instead of this I shall make an attempt at using the concept of libido for the purpose of throwing light upon group psychology, a concept which has done us such good service in the study of the psychoneuroses" (p. 90). The oedipal half of his plan then waits nearly three full chapters before it comes forward. In the interim, consideration is given to topics like the libidinal economics of Church and Army and the underside of jealousy and resentment that Freud finds beneath the conscious group tie. But when we come at last to "Identification," the subject matter and title of chapter seven, the figure of the father steps front and center from the very first paragraph:

> Identification is known to psycho-analysis as the earliest expression of an emotional tie with another person. It plays a part in the early history of the Oedipus complex. A little boy will exhibit a special interest in his father; he would like to grow like him and be like him,

and take his place everywhere. We may simply say that he takes his father as his ideal. This behavior has nothing to do with a passive or feminine attitude towards his father (and toward males in general); it is on the contrary typically masculine. It fits in very well with the Oedipus complex, for which it helps to prepare the way.

At the same time as this identification with his father, or a little later, the boy has begun to develop a true object-cathexis towards his mother according to the attachment [anaclitic] type. He then exhibits, therefore, two psychologically distinct ties: a straightforward sexual object-cathexis towards his mother and an identification with his father which takes him as a model. The two subsist side by side for a time without any mutual influence or interference. In consequence of the irresistible advance towards a unification of mental life, they come together at last; and the normal Oedipus complex originates from their confluence. The little boy notices that his father stands in his way with his mother [p. 105].

"Identification" has been given a surprisingly major role in these remarks, and its own developmental root. That said, Oedipus is now finally on board along with libido. Between these two interpretive lines, Oedipus and the libido, we expect the argument to take its predictable course—and I invite the reader to pause here and imagine for a moment how he or she thinks it will go. As for all the points that Freud has been accumulating up to now, we can be confident that he will play them out like dominoes, not by tipping them over into one another as a child does, but as a master does, placing them calmly and deliberately, one by one, in the sequence he has planned, while the other side looks on without a play.

But there are two huge and unexpected wrinkles in the argument. Libido is involved, to be sure, but it is not the ordinary kind. Central to Freud's analysis is, rather, a different kind, an aim-inhibited kind. He is explicit about this and expends long passages on it. And these passages in turn take us to a central concern of the text, the ego ideal, a concept that on first acquaintance seems to take us quite far from the primitive and unruly side of mental life. For a psychoanalytic concept, it seems almost presentable in polite company. As regards the libido, then, the text is relatively vanilla compared with what one might have expected. As for the father, it is the father of the primal horde who is at stake, when finally we get around to him, not the oedipal one. Freud is clear and enormously expansive about this, too. This material takes the tone of the text in a decidedly different direction, life in the primal horde being anything but vanilla to hear Freud tell it. The final twists and turns of the argument, to take one last look ahead, finishes up by very nearly canceling out Freud's right to speak on this topic at all—thus undoing the good work of the early pages—though perhaps only a logician spots the contradiction with which the text ends. As for the dominoes Freud has stored up to play at the end, these do meet their destined fate, but not before a good number of additional points have been made and also set aside for the grand finale. All in all, an object lesson in why one should read a text, not guess at it.

IV

It no doubt surprises the reader to hear that much of the second half of the text is taken up with "sexual instincts which are inhibited in their aim" (pp. 139, passim), to use one of the ways Freud speaks of these manifestations of the libido. In addition to what has already been noted about "identification" seemingly being given its own developmental root as a variety of "affectionate tie," Freud will contend that although most such "aim-inhibited" impulses were once more straightforwardly sexual in their aims, in the present they are not necessarily free to go back that way. Thus, not only aim inhibited and not seeking consummation now, but also aim inhibited and not seeking consummation henceforth.

If the reader is surprised, Freud himself appears to be surprised. Indeed, he cannot even begin his exposition of this side of mental life without pausing for the following, which entails in every way a great shift in tone from the measured expository melodies heard up to this point. It comes on the very next page after he has introduced "libido" as his interpretive line of approach:

> We are of the opinion . . . that language has carried out an entirely justifiable piece of unification in creating the word "love" with its numerous uses, and that we cannot do better than take it as the basis of our scientific discussions and expositions as well. By coming to this decision, psycho-analysis has let loose a storm of indignation, as though it had been guilty of an act of outrageous innovation. . . .

The majority of "educated" people have regarded this nomen-
clature as an insult and have taken their revenge by retorting upon
psycho-analysis with the reproach of "pan-sexualism." Anyone
who considers sex as something mortifying and humiliating to
human nature is at liberty to make use of the more genteel expressions "Eros" and "erotic." I might have done so myself from the
first and thus spared myself much opposition. But I did not want to,
for I like to avoid concessions or faintheartedness. One can never
tell where that road may lead one; one gives way first in words, and
then little by little in substance too. I cannot see any merit in being
ashamed of sex; the Greek word "Eros," which is to soften the
affront, is in the end nothing more than a translation of our German
word *Liebe* [love]; and finally, he who knows how to wait need
make no concessions [p. 91].

This is more than an interruption. We are being put on notice. If what
immediately follows in the text is vanilla, which only Freud knows at this
point, it will be served with gloves off.

The only comparable outburst, if I may digress for a moment, comes
but four pages later, again rather before Freud has arrived at what seems
to have provoked him. During the discussion of the libidinal ties to be
found in Church and Army, with which the second half of the text begins,
and as prelude to a discussion on panic, Freud turns almost inadvertently
to the subject of the recent Axis defeat, attributed to the "lack of psychology" in the Prussian army, that is, the failure to show the love for the
follower required of the leader. Then he blows. The outburst finishes with:

If the importance of the libido's claims on this score had been better
appreciated, the fantastic promises of the American President's
Fourteen Points would probably not have been believed so easily,
and the splendid instrument [the army] would not have broken in
the hands of the German leaders [p. 95].

In the English edition, this passage took cover in a footnote.

To return to the text, which itself returns to "at ease," the argument is
all Church and Army in this section. That the tie that binds the members
is libidinal is argued on various grounds, with Freud taking the stance that

nothing else but "love" could divert individuals from their usual pursuit of their self-interest. The most intriguing facet of the argument revolves around the phenomenon of panic as it appears on a field of battle. Here Freud finishes with McDougall:

> McDougall has even made use of panic (though not of military panic) as a typical instance of that intensification of emotion by contagion ("primary induction") on which he lays so much emphasis. But nevertheless this rational method of explanation is here quite inadequate. The very question that needs explanation is why the fear has become so gigantic. The greatness of the danger cannot be responsible, for the same army which now falls victim to panic may previously have faced equally great or greater danger with complete success. . . . If an individual in panic fear begins to be solicitous only on his own account, he bears witness in so doing to the fact that the emotional ties, which have hitherto made the danger seem small to him, have ceased to exist. Now that he is by himself in facing the danger, he may surely think it greater. The fact is therefore, that panic fear presupposes a relaxation in the libidinal structure of the group and reacts to that relaxation in a justifiable manner, and the contrary view—that the libidinal ties of the group are destroyed owing to fear in the face of the danger—can be refuted. . . .
>
> Anyone who, like McDougall, describes a panic as one of the plainest functions of the "group mind," arrives at the paradoxical position that this group mind does away with itself in one of its most striking manifestations. It is impossible to doubt that panic means the disintegration of a group; it involves the cessation of all the feelings of consideration which the members of the group otherwise show one another [pp. 96–97].

From here, Freud delineates how a member of Church or Army is twice tied emotionally—to fellow members and to the leader (in the Church, Jesus Christ). But there is an obvious difficulty here with the libidinal interpretaton of these ties, and Freud gets to it before the reader has time to think it up on his or her own, namely, that we find no frankly sexual ties, not sanctioned at any rate, in either the Church or in the Army. This is how aim-inhibited libido, barely mentioned before, makes its real debut in the argument:

> Our interest now leads us on to the pressing question as to what may be the nature of these ties which exist in groups. In the psycho-analytic study of neuroses we have hitherto been occupied almost exclusively with ties with objects made by love instincts which still pursue directly sexual aims. In groups there can evidently be no question of sexual aims of that kind. We are concerned here with love instincts which have been diverted from their original aims, though they do not operate with any less energy on that account. Now, within the range of the usual sexual object-cathexis, we have already observed phenomena which represent a diversion of the instinct from its sexual aim. We have described them as degrees of being in love [p. 103].

"Being in love" has also entered the argument—for the express purpose of rescuing the notion of "love instincts that have been diverted from their original aims." Curious. But before Freud can explicate the connection as fully as he or the reader might like, he must first take up the subject of "identification," another way in which a libidinal tie diverted from any kind of consummatory goal can be formed. Why "identification" must be laid in first becomes clear only in good time; for now the reader must wait and trust in the order in which the ship is being stocked for the voyage.

In "Identification," the chapter that supervenes, Freud has much to say, beginning with the boy's tie to his father; quoted earlier, continuing through the various ways identification can combine with, or substitute for, or assist various franker strivings after objects; and finally ending up in a brief discussion of the "ego ideal" as previously developed in his papers "On Narcissism" (Freud, 1914) and "Mourning and Melancholia" (Freud, 1917):

> On previous occasions we have been driven to the hypothesis that some such agency develops in our ego which may cut itself off from the rest of the ego and come into conflict with it. We have called it the "ego ideal," and by way of functions we have ascribed to it self-observation, the moral conscience, the censorship of dreams,

and the chief influence in repression. We have said that it is heir to the original narcissism in which the childish ego enjoyed self-suf-ficiency; it gradually gathers up from the influences of the environ-ment the demands which that environment makes upon the ego and which the ego cannot always rise to; so that a man, when he cannot be satisfied with his ego itself, may nevertheless be able to find satisfaction in the ego ideal which has been differentiated out of the ego [p. 110].

"Identification" and the "ego ideal" both on board, Freud returns to being "in love." His explication of it as being, in the main, aim inhibited is disarmingly practical minded:

In one class of cases being in love is nothing more than object-cathexis on the part of the sexual instincts with a view to directly sexual satisfaction, a cathexis which expires, moreover, when this aim has been reached; this is what is called common, sensual love. But, as we know, the libidinal situation rarely remains so simple. It was possible to calculate with certainty upon the revival of the need which had just expired; and this must no doubt have been the first motive for directing a lasting cathexis upon the sexual object and for "loving" it in the passionless intervals as well [p. 111].

In general, Freud's attitude on the pragmatics of the matter are not dissimilar from those of working-class mothers who counsel their daugh-ters that, if the boy really loves you, then he will still love you if you say no. Actually, Freud, being the better psychologist still, is of the opinion, surely correct, that the boy will love you more, that is if he loves you at all. And this gives him the key to two outstanding puzzles in the text:

In connection with this question of being in love we have always been struck by the phenomenon of sexual overvaluation—the fact that the loved object enjoys a certain amount of freedom from criticism, and that all its characteristics are valued more highly than those of people who are not loved, or than its own were at a time when it itself was not loved. If the sensual impulses are more or less effectively repressed or set aside, the illusion is produced that the object has come to be sensually loved on account of its spiritual merits, whereas on the contrary these merits may really only have been lent to it by its sensual charm.

The tendency which falsifies judgment in this respect is that of *idealization*. But now it is easier for us to find our bearings. We see that the object is being treated in the same way as our own ego, so that when we are in love a considerable amount of narcissistic libido overflows on to the object. It is even obvious in many forms of love-choice, that the object serves as a substitute for some unattained ego ideal of our own. We love it on account of the perfections which we have striven to reach for our own ego, and which we should now like to procure in this roundabout way as a means of satisfying our narcissism.

If the sexual overvaluation and the being in love increase even further, then the interpretation of the picture becomes still more unmistakable. The impulsions whose trend is toward directly sexual satisfaction may now be pushed into the background entirely, as regularly happens, for instance, with a young man's sentimental passion; the ego becomes more and more unassuming and modest, and the object more and more sublime and precious, until at last it gets possession of the entire self-love of the ego, whose self-sacrifice thus follows as a natural consequence. The object has, so to speak, consumed the ego . . . .

This happens especially easily with love that is unhappy and cannot be satisfied; for in spite of everything each sexual satisfaction always involves a reduction in sexual overvaluation. Contemporaneously with this "devotion" of the ego to the object, which is no longer to be distinguished from a sublimated devotion to an abstract idea, the functions allotted to the ego ideal entirely cease to operate. The criticism exercised by that agency is silent; everything that the object does and asks for is right and blameless. Conscience has no application to anything that is done for the sake of the object; in the blindness of love remorselessness is carried to the pitch of crime. The whole situation can be completely summarized in a formula: *The object has been put in the place of the ego ideal* [pp. 112–113].

It remains only to fit the key into the locks. There are two locks. First is the hypnotic tie, which is identical to the group tie:

The hypnotic relation is the unlimited devotion of someone in love, but with sexual satisfaction excluded; whereas in the actual case of being in love this kind of satisfaction is only temporarily kept back, and remains in the background as a possible aim at some later time.

But on the other hand we may also say that the hypnotic relation is (if the expression is permissible) a group formation with two members. Hypnosis is not a good object for comparison with a group formation, because it is truer to say that it is identical with it. Out of the complicated fabric of the group it isolates one element for us—the behavior of the individual to the leader. Hypnosis is distinguished from a group formation by this limitation of number, just as it is distinguished from being in love by the absence of directly sexual trends. In this respect it occupies a middle position between the two.

It is interesting to see that it is precisely those sexual impulses that are inhibited in their aims which achieve such lasting ties between people. But this can easily be understood from the fact that they are not capable of complete satisfaction, while sexual impulsions which are uninhibited in their aims suffer an extraordinary reduction through the discharge of energy every time the sexual aim is attained. It is the fate of sensual love to become extinguished when it is satisfied; for it to be able to last, it must from the beginning be mixed with purely affectionate components—with such, that is, as are inhibited in their aims—or it must itself undergo a transformation of this kind [p. 115].

And opening this lock puts us in view of the more important one, the nature of the tie to the leader and its role in the identification of each member with the next:

[W]e are quite in a position to give the formula for the libidinal constitution of groups, or at least of such groups as we have hitherto considered—namely those that have a leader and have not been able by means of too much "organization" to acquire secondarily the characteristics of an individual. *A primary group of this kind is a number of individuals who have put one and the same object in the place of their ego ideal and have consequently identified themselves with one another in their ego* [p. 116].

The formula is delivered with great finality, in italics, at the end of the chapter on "Being in Love and Hypnosis," very much a QED. It is this formula that Freud has been preparing us for. And though immediately he professes to see weaknesses in it, it is this formula that will stand hereafter in the text as the rule.

Yet it is a rule that is about take on, and keep, a dark coloration. Here we come to the second great and surprising wrinkle in Freud's argument. The question before the house is and has been: What is the basis of the tendency of an individual to become so involved with the group? Put alternatively: What is the valence of the group for the individual, the thing about it that pulls the individual in? If we now reframe this question according to the rule that Freud has just announced with such finality, we must ask what is it about the leader that brings out so startling a reaction from the individual. What about the follower makes him or her ready to put the leader in place of his or her ego ideal? Here it would be easy to turn to the nursery, to the idealized father, and to the vicissitudes of the father's progressive dethronement and enshrinement as the child progresses through the Oedipus. The argument almost writes itself.

But Freud does not make that argument. Instead he undertakes a descent into the underside of group dynamics starting with a consideration of Trotter's thesis of a "herd instinct." For Trotter (1916), mankind's abiding impulse toward association ("gregariousness") is an instinct, meaning that it is innate, psychologically irreducible, and coequal with self-preservation, nourishment, and sex. Freud's rebuttal depends chiefly on various demonstrations that the apparent developmental emergence of group feeling in a child is forced from without and amounts to a reaction formation. Two of the demonstrations:

> The elder child would certainly like to put his successor jealously aside, to keep it away from the parents, and to rob it of all its privileges; but in the face of the fact that this younger child (like all that come later) is loved by the parents as much as he himself is, and in consequence of the impossibility of his maintaining his hostile attitude without damaging himself he is forced into identifying himself with the other children. So there grows up in the troop of children a communal or group feeling, which is then further developed at school. The first demand made by this reaction-formation is for justice, for equal treatment for all. We all know how

loudly and implacably this claim is put forward at school. If one cannot be the favorite oneself, at all events nobody else shall be the favorite [p. 120].

It is not the case merely that the group spirit is sickly overed by such reaction-formations in Freud's telling; the group spirit is actually based on this repressed hostility, which is its true ontogenetic root:

> What appears later on in society in the shape of *Gemeingeist, espirit de corps,* "group spirit," etc., does not belie its derivation from what was originally envy. No one must want to put himself forward, every one must be the same and have the same. Social justice means that we deny ourselves many things so that others may have to do without them as well [pp. 120–121].

It is the forceful leader who keeps the whole thing from dissolving back into something far nastier, more brutish, and shorter:

> We have already heard in the discussion of the two artificial groups, Church and army, that their necessary precondition is that all their members should be loved in the same way by one person, the leader. Do not let us forget, however, that the demand for equality in a group applies only to its members and not to the leader. All the members must be equal to one another, but they all want to be ruled by one person. Many equals, who can identify themselves with one another, and a single person superior to them all—that is the situation that we find realized in groups which are capable of subsisting [p. 121].

And now Freud finishes his look at the underside of group spirit with a turn of phrase so fine as to explain why he has waited this long to take up Trotter, who as easily could have come with McDougall and Le Bon much earlier. The future Goethe Award winner, it appears, wanted to reserve the following climax for this place in his text:

> Let us venture, then, to correct Trotter's pronouncement that man is a herd animal and assert that he is rather a horde animal, an individual creature in a horde led by a chief [p. 121].

V

We are coming to our final destination—the primal horde. Freud begins the last leg of his argument amiably enough by recalling a reviewer who once called the theory a "Just So Story." But Freud is entirely serious about it. It is the primal horde, as phylogenetic inheritance, that provides the ultimate answer to our question: What is it about the group, and about the leader, that pulls the individual in?

> Thus the group appears to us as the revival of the primal horde. Just as primitive man survives potentially in every individual, so the primal horde may arise once more out of any random collection; in so far as men are habitually under the sway of group formation we recognize in it the survival of the primal horde. We must conclude that the psychology of groups is the oldest human psychology; what we have isolated as individual psychology, by neglecting all traces of the group, has only since come into prominence out of the old group psychology, by a gradual process which may still, perhaps, be described as incomplete. We shall later venture upon an attempt at specifying the point of departure of this development [p. 123].

Here we must pause, for the passage is not so transparent as the modern reader may assume (and the promised addendum about "the point of departure" for individual development, when it comes at text's end, is likely to be totally opaque). What Freud is assuming, and his readers of that time are assuming along with him, is that 19th- and early 20th-century science (in the form of an amalgam of disciplines ranging from philology and comparative mythology to anthropology, psychology, and psychiatry) has cracked the case and knows, more or less as a fact, that earliest man was possessed of, and by, a wholly communal mentality. This purely communal period is the time before time that gave us the oldest strata of mythology, myths of the Great Mother and later of a Father God. The themes of such myths, appropriately, are creation and the beginning of "the people." That group consciousness came first was the scholarly consensus. The consensus was about to crumble as progress was made in a number of disciplines, but Freud can scarcely be blamed for not seeing that coming. It was further assumed that the subsequent emergence of the self-conscious individual as a psychological possibility could be "dated," so to speak, to a somewhat more recent paleohistorical period in which was laid down the mythological strata containing the first myths of the Hero. This period is intermediate between our time, when psychological individuals are assumed—and assumed to be what psychology studies for the most part—and an archaic time when all mentality was communal.

What Freud is about to add to the prevailing consensus, beside the suggestion that our evolution beyond the communal mentality of our forebearers may be incomplete, is his own intermediate stage. This stage is defined by the mentality of the primal horde, vestiges of which, according to Freud, still animate group life. Freud's writing is surprisingly vivid. In the horde, the father, but only the father, possessed individuality. Freud seems almost to have known him:

> [T]he Father of the primal horde was free. His intellectual acts were strong and independent even in isolation, and his will needed no reinforcement from others. . . . [H]e loved no one but himself, or other people only in so far as they served his needs. . . .
>
> He, at the very beginning of the history of mankind, was the "superman" whom Nietzsche only expected from the future [p. 123].

As for what life was like, Freud's description remains vivid. "Just So Story" or not, he seems almost to have been there:

> The primal father of the horde was not yet immortal, as he later became by deification. If he died, he had to be replaced; his place was probably taken by a youngest son, who had up to then been a member of the group like any other. There must therefore be a possibility of transforming group psychology into individual psychology; a condition must be discovered under which such a transformation is easily accomplished, just as it is possible for bees in a case of necessity to turn a larva into a queen instead of into a worker. One can imagine only one possibility: the primal father had prevented his sons from satisfying their directly sexual impulses; he forced them into abstinence and consequently into the emotional ties with him and with one another which could arise out of those of their impulses that were inhibited in their sexual aim. He forced them, so to speak, into group psychology. His sexual jealousy and

intolerance became in the last resort the causes of group psychology
[p. 124].

Freud's metaphor is difficult. What the primal father gives his followers,
abstinence, is rather the opposite of royal jelly: it keeps them from
becoming queens. What is implied is that, after his death, freedom to
copulate served as royal jelly. Apart from the metaphor, there are lots of
new details here. For example, that it was the "youngest son" who
succeeded the leader is new; it is not mentioned in *Totem and Taboo*
(Freud, 1913). That the sons were forced into abstinence is not new, but
that this deprivation forced them into emotional ties with one another is
new. And so forth.

But let us not lose sight of the main argument. The tendency to involve
oneself in the group, to put oneself at the disposal of the leader—more
properly to put the leader in the place of one's ego ideal—and in so doing
to become identified with other followers, and to regress in the process,
this is all part of the archaic heritage. To repeat, "insofar as men are
habitually under the sway of group formation we recognize in it the
survival of the primal horde" (p. 123).

Freud is not entirely done. For reasons of logical completeness, he feels
he has to link the phenomenology of hypnotism to a revival of the figure
of the primal father behind the hypnotist. And for reasons not so clear, he
also feels obliged to speak a bit further on the general topic of the ego
ideal. But the argument is made.

VI

It is not an easy text to get hold of. For the contemporary reader crucial
concepts are unfamiliar, to a degree surprising given that this is, after all,
a book written by Freud. Regarding one of these concepts, sexual instincts
that are inhibited in their aims, Freud appears to be aware, at least, of a
difficulty. In his "Postscript," he mentions it: "A great deal has been said
in this paper about directly sexual instincts and those that are inhibited in
their aims, and it may be hoped that this distinction will not meet with too
much resistance" (p. 137). The concession is worth noting. Worth noting,
too, is the clue, if that's what it is, into the genesis of the work. For here
Freud writes "paper" instead of "text" or "book" or "volume." It may be
that the choice of words is a survival from the first little paper Freud wrote

after his "chance idea," which only later turned into the present work. In which case, surprisingly, instincts inhibited in their aims were part of the original inspiration.

Also worth noting is that, once again, as he did earlier, upon recognizing what he has been writing about Freud appears to gag. His turn to the topic, he right away assures the reader, in no way means that he is not aware of the originally sexual nature of such ties. Then this paragraph, all by itself, appears:

> A psychology which will not or cannot penetrate the depths of what is repressed regards affectionate emotional ties as being invariably the expression of impulses which have no sexual aim, even though they are derived from impulses which have such an aim [p. 138].

That hiss is for Alfred Adler.

Two other concepts crucial to the exposition are "identification" and the "ego ideal." Here the problem for contemporary readers is not that we are unaccustomed to hearing Freud theorize in these terms. The problem is that we are all too accustomed to them—in a different venue. Both are taken up in Freud's (1923) next major metapsychological work, *The Ego and the Id,* and it is that work with which the clinician and the general reader both are more likely to be familiar. In that work, "identification" is derived from oral object cathexes. More importantly, in that work the concept of the ego ideal is dislodged by a virtual synonym, the "superego," which thereafter becomes the term of preference, even if it means almost the same thing.

There is a slight difference: unlike the ego ideal, the superego *is* derived from the Oedipus complex, indeed is "heir" to it (p. 48). It contains not only the wish to be like the father, but also the prohibition against being like him in certain respects. The ego ideal, by contrast, though it is modified by identification with the father, is already present in Freud's (1921) account prior to the Oedipus. It is "heir" to the child's original narcisissm (p. 110). The ontogenetic difference is subtle, but it can be argued that it does affects Freud's usage—and our reading. The bigger obstacle for the reader remains his or her sheer familiarity and comfort with the newer term "superego." Using the older one "ego ideal" to steer by, Freud seems a few degrees off of true North. This, obviously, is no fault of Freud's.

Then there is the primal horde. Modern readers don't really cotton to the primal father, and their eyes tend to glaze over when they come to passages indicating that, in the unconscious at any rate, he is back. But Freud is in deadly earnest about the primal father. In the "Postscript" he returns again to life in the primal horde with a lengthy passage that specifically mentions that it has been inspired by Rank, who also appears to have been there.

The burden of this passage is nothing less than to identify the step whereby someone other than the primal father, or one of his successors in the role, achieved individuality. That person turns out to have been the first poet, who authored the first myth of the Hero, which was probably based on that youngest son mentioned earlier, "the mother's favorite, whom she had protected from paternal jealousy, and who, in the era of the primal horde, had been the father's successor" (p. 136). The myth of the Hero is the means whereby its author, and also his audience, could extract a sense of individuality, by imaginatively identifying with the Hero, from the psychology of the group. This development makes the poet, though obviously not the King, something more than the Jack, and just maybe the Ace. From here, Freud extends his analysis both backward and forward in prehistoric, that it is to say primal, time.

The passage is not easy to follow, by any means, and I have treated only the hub of it. Again, it would be easier if we were more familiar with the consensus then reigning on the arrangement of the mythic strata and its presumptive consequences for understanding man's prehistory. There is no space for it, unfortunately. And with that regret, I will break off any further attempt at either précis or exegesis save for noting a single additional suggestion of Freud (and Rank) that is also radical in an unappreciated way. If the emergence of the poet is a definite event that made its own mark in the mythic record, then all the myths would have had to be rearranged subsequently to accommodate the poet's innovation of the saga of the Hero. Thus, the mythic archive is itself out of order, thrown askew by a poetic development to be found only in Freud's chronology of the continued evolution of the primal horde. Or so it is argued. A different sort of QED, one that modern readers would likely be impatient with if they understood it better but also, in a postmodern way, might quite possibly intrigued by.

The convolutions of life in the primal horde aside, the "Postscript" is gemlike. Freud consistently finds fresh things to say, even to the point of setting his own argument at risk. In particular, he points out that neurosis entails sexual impulses that are repressed but active or, of special moment here, instincts of an aim-inhibited nature whose inhibition is shaky and coming undone. In either case, there is less energy for group involvement:

> It is in accordance with this that a neurosis should make its victim asocial and should remove him from the usual group formations. It may be said that a neurosis has the same disintegrating effect upon a group as being in love. On the other hand it appears that where a powerful impetus has been given to group formation neuroses may diminish and at all events temporarily disappear. Justifiable attempts have also been made to turn this antagonism between neuroses and group formation to therapeutic account. Even those who do not regret the disappearance of religious illusions from the civilized world of to-day will admit that so long as they were in force they offered those who were bound by them the most powerful protection against the danger of neurosis. Nor is it hard to discern that the ties that bind people to mystico-religious or philosophico-religious sects and communities are expressions of crooked cures of all kinds of neuroses [p. 142].

The same setting off of neurosis to one side occurs again at the very end of the text, where Freud closes with a lucid description of different states of mind as seen from the vantage point of libido theory:

> *Being in love* is based on the simultaneous presence of directly sexual impulsions and of sexual impulsions that are inhibited in their aims, while the object draws a part of the subject's narcissistic ego-libido to itself. It is a condition in which there is only room for the ego and the object.
>
> *Hypnosis* resembles being in love in being limited to these two persons, but it is based entirely on impulsions that are inhibited in their aims and puts the object in the place of the ego ideal.
>
> *The group* multiplies this process; it agrees with hypnosis in the nature of the instincts which hold it together, and in the replacement of the ego ideal by the object; but to this it adds identification with other individuals, which was perhaps originally made possible by their having the same relation to the object.

Both states, hypnosis and group formation, are an inherited deposit from the phylogenesis of the human libido—hypnosis in the form of a predisposition, and the group, besides this, as a direct survival. The replacement of the directly sexual impulsions by those that are inhibited in their aims promotes in both states a separation between the ego and the ego ideal, a separation with which a beginning has already been made in the state of being in love.

Neurosis stands outside this series. It also is based upon a peculiarity in the development of the human libido—the twice repeated start made by the directly sexual function, with an intervening period of latency. To this extent it resembles hypnosis and group formation in having the character of a regression, which is absent from being in love. It makes its appearance wherever the advance from the directly sexual instincts to those that are inhibited in their aims has not been wholly successful; and it represents a *conflict* between those portions of them which, springing from the repressed unconscious, strive—as do other, completely repressed, instinctual impulses—to attain direct satisfaction. Neuroses are extraordinarily rich in content, for they embrace all possible relations between the ego and the object—both those in which the object is retained and others in which it is abandoned or erected inside the ego itself—and also the conflicting relations between the ego and its ego ideal [pp. 142–143].

VII

It is an odd finale. Let us remember the start—and the reader's initial misapprehension. The phenomena of group behavior, more properly of mass behavior, seem to be natural territory for a psychologist of Freud's acuity and, most especially, with his ken for the darker recesses of human nature. One would expect the theorist of neurosis, and of the irrational in the individual mind generally, to be tempted by the various kinds of irrationalities we see in crowds, in mass movements, and, around the edges, in most forms of collective association. But the argument does not go the way one might expect. In the end, moreover, the theorist of the neurosis cancels out his own standing. For neurosis, he concludes, is a thing entirely apart. It has no role in group behavior. It is totally different in its nature.

Here the logician in the house might well beg for the floor. Is not the worth of libido theory predicated on its value in explicating the motivational structure of neurosis? If the two are things apart, if neurosis and group behavior are wholly separate, then by what warrant do we apply libido theory to the latter? Freud could reply that libido theory can also explicate the motivational structure of the group, as *Group Psychology* has shown. The logician might reply that this expanded libido theory has expanded too far to be called that if it now accepts libidinal impulses that are not, as it were, libidinous. Yet they once were libidinous, insists Freud, and that makes all the difference. Genetic fallacy, the logician answers back. And off they go, in a tango of something like a negative group formation of two.

We can eschew the tango. For myself, I take the logician's side, not that it matters. I also suspect that Freud does, too; hence his shows of defiance at times when "impulses that are inhibited in their aims" come up, again not that it matters. For, and this is one of the secrets of the book, the various ties that hold the group together need not be "libidinal" other than by fiat, and yet the psychology mostly holds good. Other motivational systems will do as well, as long as they are pressing when active, capable of enduring quietly in favoring circumstance and expressible in complementary roles.

Not only can other motivational systems be invoked, but other dynamics can be imagined as well. One can expand the text in multiple ways. In particular, the road to what is now called object relations seems wide open. For various reasons, not least among them his particular interest in the issues and his close personal friendship with Wilfred Trotter, Ernest Jones was in a sterling position to assess this work. Yet, throughout volume 3 of the *Life and Work* he silently avoids it. He gives it only the mandatory summary. That, however, is excellent, as good as one can do in two pages. In its last paragraph, the work of expansion has already begun:

> The second half of the book was taken up with the new ideas about the psychology of the ego which Freud was to expound more fully a couple of years later in The Ego and the Id. In the present connection the important point was his insistence that the ideal put forward by the leader must have a close correspondence with the ego ideal of his follower. The oscillating relations between the ego and the ego ideal, which are brought about by the restrictions this

forces on the ego, account for the various instabilities and changes to be observed in the life of groups [Jones, 1957, p. 339].

If Freud saw the room for expansion, it is unrecorded. For his own part, he soon grew unhappy with the book and declared himself dissatisfied two years later in a letter to Ferenczi. Grosskurth (1991) paraphrases thus: "As for Group Psychology . . . he now pronounced it banal, lacking clarity, and badly written" (p. 129).

The person who arguably got the most out of the text in the short term was its translator. It is not customary to connect *Group Psychology and the Analysis of the Ego* with Strachey's (1934) seminal paper on mutative interpretation entailing the internalization of the analyst by the patient as a more benign superego. Yet what is the superego but the ego ideal, and what is the analytic dyad but a group of two? Strachey might be pleased to know that, while his translating is under fire, his theory of therapy now enjoys impressive empirical validation. Of course, to claim this, he would have to allow some word changes. What the research demonstrates is that the benefit received correlates most highly with the reported internalization of the therapist as a supportive internal figure who can be consulted with imaginatively by the patient in times of distress (Wzontek, Geller, and Farber, 1995). I don't think the translator would mind putting it this way.

Grosskurth (1991), writing as a historian, has tried to expand the text in quite a different and arguably darker way. As with all historical conjectures about the genesis of this particular book, she cannot prove hers. But hers is an intriguing idea. She wonders if Freud did not mean *Group Psychology* partly as a message to his Committee, up and running since the end of the Great War and beginning to feud about how they should properly act. Hence, its distribution just prior to the 1921 meeting in the Harz mountains.

Hard to know. The Committee was Freud's Church and Army. And such a communication would have been in keeping with Freud's leadership style, which entailed continuing analysis along with considerable expectation. Still, the conjecture remains unproven. If, to continue further in this vein, Freud also intended his mentions of the "youngest son" to draw attention to Rank within the circle—there is no evidence that he did—this was a mistake. The attention Rank got soon after from fellow Committee members was not what he or Freud would have wished for.

Here another expansion of the interpretive possibilites looms up. This one actually happened. Freud and Rank saw the group in terms of a father and his sons. Parricide was the worst that could happen. But a group can be mostly about the brothers, and its crime can be murder of one of them by the others. This lethality, unfortunately, was as much a part of the Committee's inheritance as its relation to Freud. The Committee was a killing machine. It was founded to kill off Freud's Gentile son, Jung. It ended killing off his Jewish one, Rank.

Groups do terrible things sometimes. Freud knows this. Let us end by taking one last look at how he knows this. As we have noted, there is something odd about the end of the text, something odd about Freud's cutting off the limb of neurosis, which we would have guessed at the outset had to be the limb he was sitting on as he chronicled the irrationality of the group. But he was not sitting on that limb, not at the end. That is the other secret of the text, and the reason it is still worth reading and pondering. He was sitting on the limb of the primal horde.

Lately, the philosopher Daniel Dennett (1995) has made a fresh stir for himself with his book *Darwin's Dangerous Idea*. The stir is based on his noting pointedly what is logically entailed in evolution seen for what it is, namely, that our notions of the good, the true, and the beautiful cannot possibly be absolutes in the sense of being valid a priori's applicable to the universe generally. They are, rather, codes or standards or preferences that have evolved only because they have favored our evolution, and been favored in our evolution, in known and unknown ways.

Freud is more Haeckelian than Darwinian—we haven't space here for the difference—but with his phylogenetic reasoning about survivals he comes out in the same place Dennett does. Only Freud's topic is groups. What he is arguing, finally, is that, no matter how we organize ourselves, no matter how carefully we attempt to rationalize, in Weber's sense, our behavior as members, and no matter how hard we try to enforce standards of accountability on leaders and members alike, there is something inherently irrational about the result. That irrationality, that unreason in Foucault's terms, derives from the fact that our predilection for groups, and our responses inside them, are the product of an evolution that cares not for Robert's Rules of Order, the Geneva Convention, or any other rational system we might seek to impose on ourselves. It is not how the thing was built, and it is not how it operates, not at its motivational core. Not in groups of two, and not in groups of two hundred million.

A scary, sobering evolutionary truth. Very much worth pondering and, in the manner of the contributors to this volume, illuminating further. This is not an easy text to be finished with.

REFERENCES

Abraham, H. & Freud, E., eds. (1965), *A Psycho-Analytic Dialogue: The Letters of Sigmund Freud and Karl Abraham, 1907–1926*. New York: Basic Books.

Dennett, D. (1995), *Darwin's Dangerous Idea: Evolution and the Meanings of Life*. New York: Simon & Schuster.

Falzeder, E. & Brabant, E., eds. (1996), *The Correspondence of Sigmund Freud and Sándor Ferenczi, Vol. 2, 1914–1919*. Cambridge, MA: Belknap Press of Harvard University Press.

Freud, S. (1913), *Totem and Taboo. Standard Edition*, 13:1–161. London: Hogarth Press, 1950.

Freud, S. (1914), *On Narcissism: An Introduction. Standard Edition*, 14:73–102. London: Hogarth Press, 1957.

Freud, S. (1917), *Mourning and Melancholia. Standard Edition*, 14:243–258. London: Hogarth Press, 1957.

Freud, S. (1921), *Group Psychology and the Analysis of the Ego. Standard Edition*, 18:69–143. London: Hogarth Press, 1955.

Freud, S. (1923), *The Ego and the Id. Standard Edition*, 19:12–66. London: Hogarth Press, 1961.

Grosskurth, P. (1991), *The Secret Ring*. Reading, MA: Addison Wesley.

Jones, E. (1957), *The Life and Work of Sigmund Freud, Vol. 3*. New York: Basic Books.

Le Bon, G. (1895), *La Psychologie des Foules*. Paris: Felix Alcan.

McDougall, W. (1920), *The Group Mind*. Cambridge, UK: Cambridge University Press.

Paskauskas, A., ed. (1993), *The Complete Correspondence Between Sigmund Freud and Ernest Jones, 1908–1939*. Cambridge, MA: Harvard University Press.

Strachey, J. (1934), The nature of the therapeutic action of psycho-analysis. In: *The Evolution of Psychoanalytic Technique*, ed. M. S. Bergmann & F. R. Hartman. New York: Basic Books, 1976, pp. 331–360.

Trotter, W. (1916), *Instincts of the Herd in Peace and War*. London: Unwin, 1923.

Wzontek, N., Geller, J. & Farber, B. (1995), Patients' posttermination representations of their psychotherapists. *J. Amer. Acad. Psychoanal.*, 23:395–410.

PART TWO

Discussion of
Group Psychology
and the Analysis
of the Ego

Freud's
Group Psychology
Background,
Significance, and
Influence

DIDIER ANZIEU

CONTEXT

A note in the *Standard Edition* tells us of the stages in the composition of Freud's essay. He mentioned its subject in a letter to Ferenczi on May 12, 1919, and in another to Eitingon on December 2 of the same year. He completed a draft between February and September 1920 and sent it to his two correspondents. The final version was set down in February and March 1921, sent to the printer on March 28, and published at the beginning of August 1921. Freud discusses this in his letter to Abraham dated August 6, 1921.

What was the background to its writing? Let us consider first the sociohistorical context. World War I had ended in the fall of 1918. The Treaty of Versailles and its associated treaties followed in 1919. The Austrian Republic was proclaimed in 1920. Freud was relieved of his wartime anxiety about his sons, who had been in peril at the front. In

---

Translated by Philip Slotkin.

Dr. Anzieu died shortly after he completed this chapter and hence was unable to supply several missing sources for citations herein. We ask the reader's understanding in this matter.

Germany, Hitler was beginning to make use of the SA (Storm Troopers), then in the process of organization. In Italy, Mussolini was inaugurating the *Fasci di Combattimento,* the Fighting Leagues that gave their name to Fascism, and officially launched the fascist party in 1921. In Russia, after the defeat of the "White" counterrevolutionary armies that marked the end of the civil war, the transformation of the local autonomous regions into Soviet Socialist Republics proceeded apace. The Austro-Hungarian Empire was dismembered, some regions becoming independent while others were annexed by neighboring states. The Treaty of Trianon (1920) deprived the country of two thirds of its territory, reducing its population from 20 million to 7,600,000. In Hungary, after the country's defeat by the Romanians and the proclamation of a soviet republic under Béla Kun, Admiral Horthy formed a reactionary government and was proclaimed Regent.

In his address on the occasion of Ferenczi's 50th birthday, Freud referred to the combined action of Ferenczi and Anton von Freund, which "would have made Budapest the analytic capital of Europe, had not political catastrophes and personal tragedy put a merciless end to these fair hopes." Von Freund died in January 1920. Ferenczi had relinquished the presidency of the IPA in October 1919 on the grounds of Hungary's isolation from contact with the rest of the world. For the duration of Béla Kun's soviet republic (from March to August 1919), Ferenczi had been assigned teaching functions at the university, where his lectures attracted a large and eager audience. Reduced in size and resources, humiliated by defeat and impoverished, Vienna languished in famine and agitation. The old structures and models were increasingly disputed, and disorder spread. This calling into question of traditional values might well have helped inspire Freud to call his own first theory into question. The era of renewal had arrived in both his city and his mind.

In 1920, too, the logician and philosopher Wittgenstein published his first work, *Tractatus Logico-Philosophicus*, in Vienna.

Let us now turn to the personal context. At the age of 64, Freud in 1920 was embarking on a process of revising his concepts and his theories. Whereas Freud's midlife crisis, occurring when he was around the age of 40, had culminated through his self-analysis in the discovery of psychoanalysis, the crisis of the onset of old age was now to have its creative effects—namely, a new rigor in his reasoning, more care in textual composition, greater abstraction of language, and increased freedom of imagination. Indeed, the last of these points scared many of Freud's followers, who, arguing that it was a consequence of aging, refused to follow him in his new intellectual adventure.

In the course of his development, Freud had the support of a united family who valued and believed in him. Having lost his father, Jakob, in 1896 and his elder half-brother, Emmanuel, in 1915, he never failed to visit his mother, Amalia (1835–1930), several times a week. He could depend at all times on his wife, Martha, and her sister, Minna. He had six grown children, the oldest of whom were married and themselves parents. In the same year, 1920, Martin married and Sophie died of pneumonia, leaving two orphans, one of whom was the little inventor of the reel game. Freud's youngest child, Anna, was 24, and her father was beginning to worry about the absence of an appropriate suitor for her.

Moscovici (1991) draws a parallel between Freud and Einstein, who had expanded his physics of Special Relativity into the General Theory in 1919. Einstein was awarded the Nobel prize for physics in 1921, whereas Freud was hoping to receive the Nobel prize for medicine. A stimulating exchange of letters took place on the subject between the two great men, in which Freud congratulated the new Nobel laureate on his "happiness," and Einstein replied in the same tone that Freud, as a clear-sighted psychoanalyst, ought to know what happiness was and at what cost it was achieved. It was a failing of Freud's to complain of not enjoying the esteem and admiration he justifiably expected from his city and his colleagues.

Having completed his first psychoanalytic theory with the composition of the metapsychological texts of 1915, in the years 1920 to 1923 Freud published the three fundamental writings in which he corrected his earlier views and advanced beyond them. In *Beyond the Pleasure Principle* (Freud, 1920), he took the risk of conceiving a death drive distinct from and antithetical to libido. The essay with which we are here concerned, *Group Psychology and the Analysis of the Ego* (Freud, 1921c), in which he introduced the concepts of identification and the ego ideal, appeared in 1921. Finally, *The Ego and the Id* (Freud, 1923b) redrew the distribution of the agencies of the psychic apparatus (id, ego, and superego). *Group Psychology* was Freud's second contribution on group phenomena, coming as it did after *Totem and Taboo* (Freud, 1913), in which he borrowed from Darwin the hypothesis of a primal horde and in which the figure of the old, all-powerful father served in 1921 as a concrete foundation for the elaboration of the ego ideal, as yet merged with the superego.

What might have been Freud's personal experience of the groups he observed or perhaps belonged to? Owing to the resistance of psychoanalytic circles to any formula other than that of individual treatment, it is hard to say. It is quite likely, however, that the workings of the psychoanalytic societies and the umbrella organization of the International Psychoanalytical Association (involving internal group tensions, conflicts between individuals and ideas, splitting into subgroups, rivalries, ostracism, leadership struggles, and so on) might have furnished a reality background to Freud's reflections on group psychology.

At the time he was writing his 1921 essay, Freud had a slight difference of opinion with Karl Abraham on the functioning and organization of the psychoanalytic community, as revealed in their letters of June 21, June 27, and July 4, 1920. In addition, there was a secret committee to which Abraham, Eitingon, Ferenczi, Jones, Rank, and Sachs belonged. Its aim was to assemble a small, trusty group of analysts who would act as a kind of palace guard around Freud.

FERENCZI'S REVIEW OF FREUD'S ESSAY

In accordance with the duality of its title, Freud's essay can be read either as a contribution to group psychology or as an attempt to restructure the concept of the ego. Hence the difficulty of deciding which approach to adopt when reading it, as Sándor Ferenczi (1922) points out at the beginning of his review. He emphasizes Freud's epistemological reversal: "Scarcely had we got used to the idea that the basis for unraveling the complex phenomena of the group mind (art, religion, myth-formation, etc.) had been provided by the findings of the psychology of the individual, i.e. of psycho-analysis, when our confidence in it was shaken by the appearance of Freud's recent work on 'group psychology'" (p. 371). Ferenczi seeks in each of the three parts of his review to demonstrate the change in Freud's views.

He explains in the first part that Freud contradicts the banal idea that collective phenomena take place in a crowd—that is, within a large number of individuals. Ferenczi says that they may also occur within a small circle (for example, a family) or even in relations with a single individual. The latter situation, he notes, arises in the case of the well-known but as yet unexplained phenomena of hypnosis and suggestion:

> [Freud] traces the disposition to hypnosis back to its source in primitive humanity; in the primal horde the eye of the feared father-leader, who disposed of the power of life and death over every single one of its members, exercised over them throughout their lifetime the same paralyzing effect, inhibiting all independent action, all independent intellectual activity, that the eye of the hypnotist still exercises over his subjects to-day. The effectiveness of hypnosis is due to this fear of the hypnotist's eye [p. 372].

Ferenczi here refers to Freud's (1913) hypothesis of the father of the primal horde, put forward in *Totem and Taboo* before its reappearance in his new essay, although he does not mention that text explicitly.

Ferenczi points out that, according to Freud, suggestibility depends on the capacity to be hypnotized, which is not merely a residue of the infantile anxiety inspired by the severe father but also represents the return of emotions felt by the man in the primal horde when he encounters its redoubtable master.

Ferenczi tells us in the second part of his review that Freud's essay bears witness to "the discovery of a new stage in the development of the ego and the libido" (p. 373). This higher state of the ego, which succeeds the original narcissism of the child and of humanity, consists in the distinction between an ego still characterized by primary narcissism and an "ego ideal," which is a model set up within the self to measure all the latter's acts and qualities. The ego ideal performs important functions, such as reality testing, conscience, self-observation, and dream censorship; it is also the force responsible for the production of the "unconscious repressed," which is so important in neurotic formations.

Ferenczi thus implies that there are stages in ego development complementary to the stages of development of the libido described by Freud (1905) in his *Three Essays*. These fall between the phases of oral and anal-sadistic organization, which are substantially narcissistic, and object love proper. According to Freud, as revised and supplemented by Ferenczi, there is always a specific libidinal process, namely, identification. Objects from the external world are "incorporated" not in reality, as in the cannibalistic phase, but only in the imagination. Their properties are introjected and attributed to the ego itself. Ferenczi's modesty, coupled with his great respect for Freud's ideas, prevented him from pointing out that the latter rightly credits him with the creation of the concept of introjection, which Freud subsequently took up. Fixation to the stage of identification makes it possible to regress from the later phase of object love to the earlier state of identification. Ferenczi was led by the new conceptual tools of identification and introjection to undertake his own reworking of certain aspects of psychoanalytic theory.

Male homosexuality regresses from object love to identification: the woman is abandoned as an external love object but is introjected into the ego, that is, put in the place of the ego ideal: "Thus the male becomes feminine and seeks out another male, thereby re-establishing the original heterosexual relationship, but in reverse" (p. 374).

Ferenczi goes on to say that paranoia appears as a disorder not only of the (homosexual) relation to the father but also of (asexual) social identification: "Freud has now for the first time enabled us really to understand why so many people succumb to paranoia as a result of offenses to which they have been subjected in social life" (pp. 374–375). The libido, hitherto bound socially, finds itself liberated by the fact of the offense and seeks to express itself in a crudely sexual form—as a rule homosexual—that is suppressed by a particularly demanding ego ideal. The old social bond continues to be expressed in the delusional feeling of being persecuted by certain groups (Jesuits, Freemasons, Jews, etc.).

Melancholia proves to be the consequence of the substitution of the object of the ego ideal for the object abandoned in the outside world because it was hated.

The manic phase of cyclothymia is a temporary rebellion of the primary narcissistic ego residue against the tyranny of the ego ideal.

In hysterical identification, the unconscious incorporation of the object extends only to some of its characteristics.

In Ferenczi's view, important facets of the functioning of our love lives call for revision in the light of these new conceptions.

Increased importance attaches to the distinction between the direct and the aim-inhibited sexual drive.

The sense of shame becomes understandable when seen as determined by a phenomenon of group psychology—that is, as a reaction to the disturbance caused by the public expression of heterosexual drives, which are always asocial.

Ferenczi thus appears to be more interested in the developments in individual psychopathology furnished by Freud's propositions than in their application to social phenomena.

LE BON AND *LA PSYCHOLOGIE DES FOULES*

Le Bon's (1895) *La Psychologie des Foules* made its author famous. Freud read it, pen in hand, in its second German edition, and I contend that this experience triggered the creative process that culminated in his composition of *Group Psychology and the Analysis of the Ego*. The German translator used the word *Führer* to render the French term *meneur;* the English version is *leader* and the Spanish *líder*.

Moscovici (1991) summarizes Le Bon's life as follows:

> Gustave Le Bon was born in 1841 at Nogent-le-Rotrou in Normandy. He died in Paris in 1931 after a life that was noteworthy in many respects. Chance had it that he was born at a time when the seeds of progress were beginning to emerge. His maturity coincided with the Second Empire, a period of industrial revolution, military defeat, and civil war. Finally, he lived long enough to witness the victory of science, the crises of democracy, and the rise of socialism and popular forces, which he watched with growing concern, drawing attention to their increasing power.
>
> This provincial physician, short in stature and a lover of good food, had ceased early on to practice his art in order to devote himself to scientific popularization [p. 73f.].

Among Le Bon's principal publications were works on the civilizations of Arabia and India, *Les Lois Psychologiques de l'Évolution des Peuples* [The Psychological Laws of the Evolution of Peoples] (1894), *La Psychologie des Foules* [Crowd Psychology] (1895), and *La Psychologie Politique* [Political Psychology] (1910). Le Bon owes his reputation to the second of these books. Often republished, it was translated into 17 languages—even Arabic and Japanese. Because of his fame, this stay-at-home was visited by a constant procession of statesmen, writers, and scientists, such as Ribot, Tarde, Bergson, Henri Poincaré, Paul Valéry, Princesses Marthe Bibesco and Marie Bonaparte, Raymond Poincaré, Aristide Briand, Louis Barthou, and Theodore Roosevelt. *La Psychologie des Foules,* of all the books ever written on social psychology, remains the most influential. It evoked immediate responses, was commented upon, criticized, and "obviously plagiarized." The concepts of the *crowd* and the *group* were taken over by so-called collective psychology and political sociology. Among the best known of the political writings are Hitler's (1925) *Mein Kampf* and Charles de Gaulle's (1932) *Le Fil de l'Épée.* Notwithstanding their different and even antithetical objectives, the approaches of these two men to achieving them take account of group psychology. De Gaulle (1932), for example, wrote that the credit accorded in bygone days by the masses to office or birth is now transferred solely to those who have succeeded in asserting themselves. And although prestige includes a component that cannot be acquired but comes from the depths of the soul and varies from one individual to another, certain constant and necessary elements may nevertheless be discerned in it. It is possible to acquire or at least to develop these. As with the artist, the leader requires a talent honed by the practice of his calling.

More information can be found in Barrows (1981), who writes that

> probably no one was better suited than [Le Bon] to the dissemination of conservative ideology in the guise of objective truth. . . . Le Bon found the perfect vehicle for his pessimism and his antiegalitarianism in the study of crowds. . . . Le Bon saw the crowd as inferior and threatening. . . . why did Le Bon's book become the classic treatise of crowd psychology? . . . because he was able to forge the clearest, most comprehensive statement of collective behavior. Unencumbered with complex academic qualifications, Le Bon reduced the components of crowd theory into a taut treatise. . . . Thus Le Bon simplified crowd psychology and made it the model for group psychology.

For Gustave Le Bon, crowds were "'somewhat like the sphinx of ancient fable: it is necessary to arrive at a solution of the problems offered by their psychology or to resign oneself to being devoured by them.' Le Bon had chosen his metaphor with care. Like the crowd, the sphinx was an enigmatic and dangerous monster, half female, half beast." Le Bon dreamed of being the Oedipus of modern times.

It will come as no surprise that Freud identified with Le Bon's book.

FREUD'S CONTRIBUTION TO GROUP PSYCHOLOGY: REVISION OF HIS TOPOGRAPHY

Freud's essay comprises 12 chapters, to each of which he gave a title except for the 12th and last, the postscript, which includes five points: (a) the difference between the Church and the Army; (b) the poet's creation of the hero; (c) further comments on the importance of the aim-inhibited sexual drives; (d) the contrast between a couple and a group; and (e) further remarks on the distinction between the state of being in love and hypnosis.

In the introduction (chapter 1), a comparison between individual and social psychology provides the foundation for Freud's basic argument.

Chapter 2, "Le Bon's Description of the Group Mind," gives a detailed account of and quotes liberally from Le Bon's book, *La Psychologie des Foules*, which Freud had read. The French translation of Freud's work reproduces Le Bon's text in the form of notes, whereas Freud himself used the German version. Here are some extracts. "[The individual] is no longer himself, but has become an automaton who has ceased to be guided by his will" (p. 76). Hence the analogy with the psychic life of primitive peoples and children (the analogy between children, savages and madmen was, of course, one of the dominant ideologies in the human sciences at the beginning of the 20th century).

A group is impulsive, changeable and irritable. It is led almost exclusively by the unconscious [p. 77]. A group is extraordinarily credulous and open to influence. . . . It thinks in images, which call one another up by association [p. 78]. . . . A group, further, is subject to the truly magical power of words. . . . And . . . groups have never thirsted after truth. They demand illusions. . . . It [the group] has such a thirst for obedience that it submits instinctively to anyone who appoints himself its master [pp. 80–81].

The master operates by "prestige." The reader is thus presented with an abundance of generally accurate facts, which are not described and classified in a precise order. One gains the impression that the multitude of facts parallels the multitude of ideas.

In chapter 3, "Other Accounts of Collective Mental Life," Freud reproaches Le Bon for describing rather than explaining. He goes on to examine McDougall's (1920) *The Group Mind*. While rightly embracing McDougall's distinction between the simple "unorganized" group and highly organized groups, whose minds may attain a higher level, Freud challenges McDougall's emphasis on suggestion or "direct induction of emotion": "suggestion, which explained everything, was itself to be exempt from explanation" (p. 89).

Chapter 4, "Suggestion and Libido," offers a psychoanalytic reinterpretation, in libido terms, of the empirical observations of Le Bon and McDougall and attempts to take account more correctly of the suggestion phenomena characteristic of groups. The group is manifestly made to cohere by some power. But to what power other than Eros, which holds everything together in the world, can this feat be ascribed? The essence of the group mind is love relationships, or, in other words, emotional ties. Freud thus argues along lines similar to those of the Marxists or structuralists: group phenomena form a superstructure, whose infrastructure is libido. He uses a technique that "denounces" what the reader thinks he knows and in fact hides the underlying processes from him. It is not enough, however, to introduce the libido without specifying the structure within which it operates; and, to grasp this structure, Freud resorts to a form of reasoning involving two apparently similar realities, the difference between which is then demonstrated. He later uses a variant on this technique in which he takes two different realities and attempts to discover the similarities between them. These two techniques are means of discovery, bringing in their wake the conviction of the investigator—that is, Freud. To secure the conviction of the reader, or interlocutor, Freud uses techniques of persuasion reminiscent of a Socratic dialogue. In the composition of his essay, he imagines his reader, whom he upbraids, imputing to him his own hesitations, ignorance, and fear of being wrong, and thereby ultimately persuading him of the truth of his theses. This makes for a very lively text: the reader is, so to speak, taken by the hand and gradually led to grasp the latent structure of the phenomena concerned. In his *Introductory Lectures on Psycho-Analysis,* Freud (1916–1917) presents his ideas in the imaginary form of a course that he never held but that the reader has the impression of attending as he reads. This technique of conviction on the part of the author and persuasion of the interlocutor seems to me to echo the processes whereby a group is held together. The stimulatory power of Freud's texts, in my view, has the same origins as those of a group's cohesion.

Chapter 5, "Two Artificial Groups: The Church and the Army," illustrates the epistemological variant mentioned earlier: Freud compares and contrasts two apparently dissimilar realities, the Church and the Army. The fundamental antithesis is between leaderless groups (for example, Le Bon's "crowd") and groups with a leader, that is, "highly organized, lasting and artificial groups." Freud sets out the psychological principle that underlies these two formations: there is "a head—in the Catholic Church Christ, in an army its Commander-in-Chief—who loves all the individuals in the group with an equal love" (p. 94). This is a "mirage" or "illusion," which can be seen as the societal illusion par excellence. The believers call themselves brothers in Christ, that is, brothers through the love that Christ has for them. There is no doubt that the tie that unites each individual with Christ is also the cause of the tie that unites them with one another. The same goes for the Army: the Commander-in-Chief is the father who loves all soldiers equally, and they are therefore "comrades" among themselves.

Freud is then able to specify an aspect of the structure within which the libido operates—its bivalence. The emotional ties have a twofold orientation, with a "vertical" element relating to the head, leader, or father, and a "horizontal" component directed toward the members of the group. Freud in this case uses a different type of argument: he suspends one component of the structure in order to examine how that structure is thereby changed. This experiment occurs involuntarily in particular circumstances, of which Freud gives two examples. The first is the war neuroses, which had caused the German army to disintegrate. These were largely a protest against the absence of love in the treatment of ordinary individuals by their superiors. A second example is panic, which "means the disintegration of a group; it involves the cessation of all the feelings of consideration which the members of the group otherwise show one another" (p. 97). Here, again, Freud reasons, as it were, from the surface down: the disintegration of the group is the manifest phenomenon, while the underlying process is the liberation of hostile impulses hitherto contained by the tie of love to the leader: "a religion, even if it calls itself the religion of love, must be hard and unloving to those who do not belong to it" (p. 98). Sustained by this principle, Freud ventures what were to prove prophetic comments: "If another group tie takes the place of the religious one—and the socialistic tie seems to be succeeding in doing so—then there will be the same intolerance towards outsiders as in the days of the Wars of Religion" (p. 99). The examples of the war neuroses and panic thus reveal a new characteristic of libidinal structure, namely, its ambivalence. It can be activated just as readily by hate as by love. In its usual condition, aggression is contained by the emotional ties with the leader, but it is unleashed if the love relationship among the individuals in the group disappears. Chapter 5 thus basically describes the psychological structure of the group in terms of its bipolarity (love of the leader and love among the members) and ambivalence (love readily turning to hostility and then to destruction).

Chapter 6, "Further Problems and Lines of Work," states that the tie with the leader is more decisive than that among the individuals making up the group and that there are leaders of a secondary type in which the person is replaced by an idea or an abstraction. Any emotional relationship between two people that lasts for some time contains a sediment of feelings of aversion and hostility, which escapes perception only as a result of repression. But what is it that sets this mechanism in motion?

Chapter 7, "Identification," shows that it is either cathexis of the object without a sexual component or identification with a model. The identification is connected with the Oedipus complex; the object cathexis toward the mother differs from the boy's identification with the father as a model. Identification with the father and an object choice relating to the father gradually come to coexist. "In the first case one's father is what one would like to *be,* and in the second he is what one would like to *have*" (p. 106). Identification aspires to give the subject's ego a form similar to that of the other's ego, taken as a "model." Identification, the most original form of emotional tie to an object, becomes a substitute for a libidinal object relationship and, by introjection of the object into the ego, can appear whenever something in common is perceived with a person toward whom sexual drives are not directed. This process underlies the genesis of male homosexuality. At puberty, instead of exchanging the mother for another sexual object, the young man identifies with her and looks about for objects that can replace his ego for him and on which he can bestow the love and care he has experienced from his mother. The second example is melancholia, which is characterized by self-depreciation of the ego, self-criticism, and self-reproach. The ego is divided into two pieces, the first of which rages against the second—that is, the one that governs the introjection of the lost object. A second develops in the ego the agency prepared to enter into conflict with the ego: "We have called it the 'ego ideal,' and by way of functions we have ascribed to it self-observation, the moral conscience, the censorship of dreams, and the chief influence in repression" (p. 110) Not long after, in *The Ego and the Id,* Freud (1923) was to distinguish the ego ideal proper, which aspires to resemble what the parents want it to be, from the superego, which lays down prohibitions and threatens punishment for disobedience. A footnote sketches out the distinction between imitation and identification; a fuller discussion is unfortunately lacking.

Identification is therefore necessary for the libidinal organization of a group.

Chapter 8, "Being in Love and Hypnosis," contains the necessary consideration of another type of relationship between the object and the ego. The child's initially sexual drives undergo repression, whereby they become "inhibited as to their aims." Affection holds sway over sensuality, which, however, continues to lead an underground existence. "The depth to which anyone is in love, as contrasted with his purely sensual desire, may be measured by the size of the share taken by the aim-inhibited instincts [drives] of affection" (p. 112). One of the characteristics of the state of being in love is sexual overvaluation, in which the narcissism of the ego is projected into the partner. The ego enriches itself with the properties of the object it "introjects"—but a problem then arises: does the object take the place of the ego or of the ego ideal? Hypnosis resembles the state of being in love by virtue of the fascination and subjection involved: "the hypnotist has stepped into the place of the ego ideal" (p. 114). The resemblance lies in the fact that the hypnotic relationship is a group formation involving two people, whereas the distinction is that the hypnotic relationship excludes directly sexual trends. This analogy confirms the primordial role of the leader, who "hypnotizes the group." Freud is now in a position to state the basic formula for the psychological structure of groups: "*A primary group of this kind is a number of individuals who have put one and the same object in the place of their ego ideal and have consequently identified themselves with one another in their ego"* (p. 116).

Chapter 9 deals with Trotter's concept of the "herd instinct," which Freud challenges.

Chapter 10, "The Group and the Primal Horde," returns to the Freudian (1913) myth of *Totem and Taboo,* attributable originally to Darwin (1871), who had postulated that the primal form of human society consisted of a horde dominated without restriction by a strong male. The group is said to be a reminiscence of the primal horde; thus, group psychology is the oldest human psychology. Individual psychology emerged only progressively and partially from it: "The primal father is the group ideal, which governs the ego in the place of the ego ideal" (p. 127).

Chapter 11 describes a "differentiating grade in the ego." The tyranny of the ego ideal over the ego gives rise to an ego reaction whereby the prohibitions are periodically infringed, as in such festivals as the Saturnalia and carnival. The tension between the ego and the ego ideal gives rise to mood swings, manifested in extreme cases in melancholia and mania. The ego and ego ideal coalesce in the manic subject, producing a mood of triumph and self-satisfaction disturbed by no self-criticism. The libidinal structure of a group regresses to a stage at which a distinction no longer obtains, on the one hand, between the ego and the ego ideal, and, on the other, between the two consequent types of link, identification and installation of the object in the place of the ego ideal.

Freud seems not to have returned to the subject of group psychology in any of his subsequent works; furthermore, he does not distinguish between small and large groups. The concept of group dynamics came into being only with Kurt Lewin, 20 years later. Freud's 1921 essay did not inspire any works on the same subject by other authors. However, present-day readers would surely wish to see the two canonical examples of the Church with its believers and the Army with its soldiers supplemented by a third, namely, the Party and its militants, including, of course, the psychology of a revolutionary party. This third group would presumably share some of the characteristics of the Church and the Army, and an examination of the differences between the Party and Freud's two groups would also be interesting. The Party promises the people happiness, just as the Church postpones the attainment of bliss to the afterlife. The presence of an Army provides necessary support for the Party's revolutionary actions, while at the same time representing a counterrevolutionary threat to the Party.

With regard to the psychic agencies, Freud was later to transform his initial distinctions among conscious, preconscious, and unconscious (which are psychic qualities and not agencies) into new and wider distinctions among agencies proper, the ego, id, superego, and ego ideal, to which some authors have suggested the addition of the ideal ego. This last distinction was to prove useful in examination of the psychic structure of small groups organized around an ideal ego, unlike the large groups considered by Freud, which are organized around the ego ideal. Psychoanalytic research and practice were, in fact, to receive a boost when they came to be directed toward small groups and no longer only large collective organizations. One exception is the institutional work of an English follower of Melanie Klein, the psychoanalyst Elliott Jaques (1951), who showed that organization and rules in industrial undertakings constitute defense mechanisms against persecutory and depressive anxieties, the importance of which in psychic functioning had been highlighted by Klein. The most original contribution was made by W. R. Bion, even though his period of group activity lasted only a few years. He was subsequently to concentrate on the individual treatment of psychotic patients.

Although each author has his own conceptual and technical variants, the basic pattern of a small psychoanalytic group may be regarded as comprising 10 or so participants, previously unknown to each other, who are invited to speak freely among themselves. These are groups with a psychotherapeutic or training intention. The leader is an analyst who interprets the group's emotions, tensions, conflicts, and the respective underlying fantasies, resistances, and so on.

AFTER FREUD (1):
BION'S "BASIC ASSUMPTIONS"

Bion (1961) transposed the rules of individual analytic treatment to the operation of a military psychiatric hospital during the World War II. Bion was in charge of a group of 400 men, who could not be treated individually and among whom a lack of discipline and laziness prevailed. He saw this attitude as a collective resistance and decided to communicate with them in words alone. He laid down a code of rules, equivalent to those of individual psychoanalysis: the men were to divide into groups; each group was to have a different activity; individuals were free to form or join a group; they could stop participating in the activity of the group provided they informed the nursing orderly before going to the rest room; and a parade or general meeting would be held every day at noon to examine the situation. Joining in a free group activity was equivalent for the community to an analysand's commitment to free association; the moral obligation to attend sessions in the one case and the meetings in the other is similar; and, finally, the invitation to say what one thinks and feels in the situation thus defined (i.e., the expression of fantasies, affects, and transference) was implicit in the practice of the daily parade, which allowed the psychiatrist to supply interpretations, where applicable, of the meaning of the group's experiences as the situation progressed. The success of this pilot experiment (the community rapidly took charge of its own affairs, doing its utmost to organize group activities intended to raise the level of personal dignity, thus speeding up the return of these unfit soldiers to active service) inspired many attempts in psychiatric hospitals at therapy by group activity (*sociotherapy*).

After the war, Bion used group psychotherapy to rehabilitate veterans and former prisoners of war and facilitate their return to civilian life. In accordance with his idea that ready-made thoughts had to be relinquished in order to approach the unconscious, Bion invented a new conceptual language. First, he distinguished two levels of functioning in small groups. The first, the work group, had to do with the conscious ego and took account of reality; such a group pursued its aims and analyzed its difficulties. The second and less accessible basic level was the unconscious "basic assumption" that underlay, or paralyzed, the work group and represented the group's fundamental experience. He distinguished three basic assumptions: dependence, fight–flight, and pairing coupled with Messianic hope. These are evidently in good agreement with the three psychological groups studied by Freud in his essay: dependence is the foundation of the Church, fight–flight is the basis of the Army, while the couple and the family are concrete manifestations of erotic desire and the expectation of a child.

Bion did not go into much detail on the nature and origin of the "basic assumptions." I imagine them as the group-process equivalent of dreams in the individual psychic process. The "basic assumption," in my view, corresponds to the latent content, whereas the collective work of association in the group is the manifest content. Interpretation should therefore proceed from the individual fantasies expressed by each participant to the "basic assumptions" common to almost all members of the group. At a given moment, the "basic assumptions" would be "dispositions to," for example, a disposition to expect everything—food, knowledge, the order of the day—from a leader. These dispositions are presumably acquired in infancy and may even be innate. Unlike fantasies, they are not derivatives of the drives but forms of emotional relationship with others, elevated into patterns of behavior. These three assumptions develop, it seems to me, in the three directions of human relationship: dependence has to do with the child's relationship with its parents and subsequently with adults in general; fight–flight as a response to enemies or rivals is connected with the child's relationship with siblings, schoolfellows, and, more generally, contemporaries; and, finally, pairing is the basis of the child's relationship with the parental couple—the wish for, or rejection of, the mutual love of father and mother, expectation of a little brother or sister, sensitivity to manifestations of affection between the parents, and so on. The "basic assumption" of pairing consists in the sense of wonder on the part of the members of the group at the birth among them of a loving couple, accompanied by the "Messianic" expectation (according to Bion) of a child, an idea, or a piece of work.

AFTER FREUD (2): THE PSYCHOANALYTIC GROUP, PSYCHOANALYTIC FAMILY PSYCHOTHERAPY, THE GROUP ILLUSION, AND THE GROUP PROCESS

The Psychoanalytic Group

The way for group psychoanalysis proper was paved before World War II by the experiences and ideas of S. H. Foulkes (1964) in England. His two principal contributions were the idea of an unconscious "resonance" between the members of the group and the recommendation that group phenomena be understood in the "here-and-now." This advice was elevated to the status of a rule by John Rickman at London's Tavistock Clinic. On this basis, Ezriel (1950) defined a group situation intended to be wholly psychoanalytic. Some eight subjects met for one hour with an analyst two or three times a week. The basic instruction was to free associate: the group members were invited to talk among themselves as spontaneously as possible about the things that came into their minds. A second rule, which followed from the fact of the existence of the group, was that, if the participants met outside the sessions, they had to report in the next session what they had said and done together (everything had to be brought back into the group). Once the treatment had begun, individual interviews were as a rule no longer granted. The analyst concentrated on the group as a whole and directed his interpretations to it alone; and these interpretations related to the current attitude of the group in the session. In other words, they were here-and-now interpretations.

When several people meet, each projects his unconscious fantasy object on to the others and attempts to make them act in accordance with it. If that member's fantasy corresponds to a fantasy of his own, each member will play the expected part and a "common group tension" will arise. If not, he will counter this tension with unconscious defense mechanisms, which will then appear. The analyst has to understand what the attitudes and thoughts of one member of the group mean to the others and how each reacts specifically to the common group problem. His interventions must be directed toward the latent problem revealed by the manifest content of the discussions—that is, the "common denominator of the dominant unconscious fantasies of the group" (p. 63). What he has to bring out in a general silence, in detailed accounts of people's lives, in idle discussions about work or literature, in jokes, in a refusal to talk in front of the others, or in the fact of someone speaking in the place of or for others are resistances to the formation of a common group tension. Finally, intragroup transferences are disregarded, only the group's transference on to the analyst being deemed meaningful.

André Ruffiot (Ruffiot et al., 1981) illustrated the specific setting of psychoanalytic family psychotherapy by showing how to transpose the rules of individual treatment to it. First, representatives of at least two generations must be present in each session; otherwise the session is canceled (owing to the need to recognize the family not only as a system in general but also as a system of fantasy transmission from generation to generation). Second, the rule of free speech is supplemented by a statement that the therapist is listening for manifestations of deep psychic life, and in particular dreams; this usually gives rise to reports of night dreams in each session, thus breaking up the vicious circle of paradox and counter-paradox. Finally, the rules of neutrality and abstinence are explicitly stated.

I, on the basis of Freud's first topography (conscious, preconscious, unconscious, and the two censorships), then postulated analogies between groups and dreams (Anzieu, 1966). Individuals expect the group to provide imaginary fulfillment of their repressed wishes; hence the frequent occurrence in groups of the allegorical themes of Paradise Lost, the discovery of an Eldorado, reconquering a holy place, or setting off on a journey to Cythera—in a word, Utopia. At the same time, anxiety and guilt feelings at transgression of a prohibition are intensified. Hence the paralyzing silence commonly encountered in sessions where people are invited to speak freely—that is, by implication, about their suppressed wishes. As a result, I used the term *group illusion* to denote a group's search for a collective fusional state: "we feel good together," "we are a good group with a good leader" (Anzieu, 1971). The latent counterpart of this manifest content is incorporation of the breast as a good part-object; partaking by all in the ideal of narcissistic omnipotence projected onto the mother/group; and hypomanic defense against the archaic fear of destruction of rivals/children in the mother's womb. At this point it proved necessary to base group work on Freud's second theory and to show the respects in which every group—from the moment of its constitution as such it ceased to be an agglomeration of individuals—is a projection and reorganization of the subjective topographies of its members. In the group illusion, the group takes the place of the ego ideal of each member, just as Freud showed that, in hierarchic collective organizations, the father imago of the leader takes the place of each individual's ego ideal.

I personally have observed that the evolution of small groups of this kind breaks down into stages. The first is characterized by the participants' as yet unconscious fragmentation and persecution anxieties. An encounter with a dozen or so unknown people arouses anxiety because it threatens the identity of each before it has been possible to establish a group unity. The participants feel threatened just as much by those who keep silent as by the ones who speak and thereby impose their views on the others.

This persecutory phase gives way to one of collective elation, in which the participants love the group and are loved by it, the leader being included in this dynamic. This is what I have called the group illusion, which constitutes a group narcissism and reverses the paranoid–schizoid anxieties into moments of euphoria and unification. Any group will create itself spontaneously if left free, forming in and through a moment of illusion. Accompanying these two crisis stages are specific fantasies characteristic of individuals in a nondirective group relationship: fantasies of damage in the initial persecutory stage and fantasy representations of the group as a mouth in the group illusion.

Once the group has been constituted psychologically in its unity and dynamism, it can set about the work of achieving its objectives and deciding on the means for their accomplishment. However, disappointment will ensue and the group illusion will be reversed into disillusionment. The differences among the individual fantasies, affects, and ideas are then exacerbated. The group becomes conscious of its inability to attain its objectives. The participants undergo the same depressive anxiety. Conflicts between individuals proliferate and intensify. The fate of the group depends on economic factors. The group may overcome the crisis of disillusionment and project its feelings of rage and hate onto an external object: the designation of an enemy for the purpose of restoring a group's unity and dynamism is a well-known phenomenon. In this way, libidinal and aggressive drives can coexist in different sectors of the group's psychic apparatus. Another possibility is that self-destructive drives may gain the upper hand, culminating in the group's eventual self-destruction.

Afterword: The Search for Eldorado— An Example of Group Process

The mirage of Eldorado captured the imagination of the writers who helped to disseminate the legend throughout Europe and adorned it with imaginary or fanciful details. The group illusion is clearly capable of fanciful elaboration that captures and incorporates many lost fantasies.

The *conquistadores* of the New World spent their energies in the quest for the silver mountains and golden-roofed cities that the tales of the Indians set in ever-more remote locations. The spoils brought back from Peru and Panama conferred retrospective legitimacy on rumors of the existence of a wondrous empire in the interior of the continent, from Peru to the River Plate. The treasures retrieved from Mexico by Cortés justified the most extravagant hopes. For that reason, no failure ever discouraged the would-be conquerors of a mythical Eldorado. And the legend of the Indian ruler whose body was plastered with gold was accompanied by a belief in the realm of the Amazons, female warriors whose name was given to the river that flows through the jungles of northern South America.

REFERENCES

Anzieu, D. (1971), L'illusion groupale. *Nouvelle Revue de Psychanalyse,* 4:73–93.

Anzieu, D. & Martin, J.-Y. (1997), *La Dynamique des Groupes Restreints,* 11th ed. Paris: Presses Universitaires de France.

Barrows, S. (1981), *Distorting Mirrors: Visions of the Crowd in Late Nineteenth Century France.* New Haven, CT: Yale University Press.

Bion, W. R. (1961), *Experiences in Groups.* London: Tavistock.

Darwin, C. (1871), *The Descent of Man, and Selection in Relation to Sex.* London: J. Murray.

De Gaulle, C. (1932), *Le Fil de l'Épée.* Paris: Berger Levrault, 1944.

Ezriel, H. (1950), A psycho-analytic approach to group treatment. *Brit. J. Med. Psychol.,* 23:59–74.

Ferenczi, S. (1922), Freud's "Group psychology and the analysis of the ego"—Its contribution to the psychology of the individual. In: *Final Contributions to the Problems and Methods of Psycho-Analysis,* ed. M. Balint (trans. E. Mosbacher). London: Karnac Books, 1980, pp. 371–376.

Foulkes, S. H. (1964), *Therapeutic Group Analysis.* London: Allen & Unwin.

Freud, S. (1905). *Three Essays on the Theory of Sexuality. Standard Edition,* 7:130–243. London: Hogarth Press, 1953.

Freud, S. (1913). *Totem and Taboo. Standard Edition,* 13:1–131. London: Hogarth Press, 1959.

Freud, S. (1916–1917), *Introductory Lectures on Psycho-Analysis. Standard Edition,* 15 & 16. London: Hogarth Press, 1963.

Freud, S. (1920), *Beyond the Pleasure Principle. Standard Edition,* 18: 7–64. London: Hogarth Press, 1955.

Freud, S. (1923), *The Ego and the Id. Standard Edition,* 19:12–66. London: Hogarth Press, 1951.

Hitler, A. (1925), *Mein Kampf.* Munich: Zentralverlag der NSDAP, 1940.

Jaques, E. (1951), *The Changing Culture of a Factory.* London: Tavistock.

Le Bon, G. (1894), *Les Lois Psychologiques de l'Évolution de Peuples.* Paris: Félix Alcan.

Le Bon, G. (1895), *La Psychologie des Foules.* Paris: Félix Alcan.

Le Bon, G. (1910), *La Psychologie Politique et la Défense Sociale.* Paris: E. Flammarion.

Lewin, K. (1947), Frontiers in group dynamics. *Field Theory in Social Science.* New York: Harper & Brothers, 1951.

McDougall, W. (1920), *The Group Mind.* Cambridge, UK: Cambridge University Press.

Moscovici, S. (1991), *L'Âge des Foules,* 2nd ed.

Ruffiot, A. et al. (1981), *La Thérapie Familiale Psychanalytique.* Paris: Dunod.

Trotter, W. (1916), *Instincts of the Herd in Peace and War.* London: Unwin, 1923.

Wittgenstein, L. (1922), *Tractatus Logico-Philosophicus.* London: K. Paul, Tronch, Trubner.

Group Psychology
and the
Psychoanalytic
Group

ROBERT CAPER

GROUP PSYCHOLOGY AND IDENTIFICATION

In *Group Psychology and the Analysis of the Ego,* Freud (1921) attempted to apply his understanding of the unconscious forces active in the mind of the individual to certain aspects of the mental life of groups. He argued vigorously and systematically that group mental life arises entirely from unconscious forces already present in the individual and that it therefore cannot be adequately understood without taking into account the individual's unconscious mental life.

This is perhaps the point that Freud's book is best known for making, but he also argued that the converse is true: that we cannot have an adequate understanding of the unconscious of the individual without taking into account the mental life of the group to which he belongs. In fact, this latter argument appears in the very first paragraph of his book:

> [O]nly rarely and under certain exceptional conditions is individual psychology in a position to disregard the relations of this individual to others. In the individual's mental life someone else is invariably involved, as a model, as an object, as a helper or as an opponent: and from the very first individual psychology, in this extended but entirely justifiable sense of the words, is at the same time social psychology as well [p. 69].

61

And again later in the book, when he writes: "[T]he psychology of groups is the oldest human psychology; what we have isolated as individual human psychology, by neglecting all traces of the group, has only since come into prominence out of the old group psychology, by a process which may still, perhaps, be described as incomplete" (p. 123).

It is the latter argument that I wish to focus on in this paper. Since Freud wrote these words, it has become clear that individual human psychology cannot be isolated from group psychology, not simply because one of the functions of the mind is to form relationships with objects, but because the individual's relationship to the object is an integral part of the mind itself. A mind without links to objects is simply not a human mind, and one simply cannot, therefore, have an adequate picture of the individual human mind without considering the links that the mind has to its objects.[1]

In *Group Psychology*, Freud approaches the indissoluble link between mind and object through a concept that he developed only a few years earlier, namely the ego ideal—something that is partly ego and partly object:

> The assumption of this kind of differentiating grade in the ego [i.e. between the ego proper and the ego ideal] as a first step in an analysis of the ego must gradually establish its justification in the most various regions of psychology. . . . Let us reflect that the ego now enters into the relationship of an object to the ego ideal which has been developed out of it, and that all the interplay between the external object and the ego as a whole, with which our study of the neuroses has made us acquainted, may possibly be repeated upon this new scene of action within the ego [p. 130].

The new scene of action is what has since come to be called the internal world or internal object world, and the means by which the repetition of the interplay between ego and external object is made possible within the ego—the means by which the ego ideal becomes possible as a hybrid of ego and object—is the ego's identification with the object.

Identification itself is a complex phenomenon. In *Group Psychology*, Freud uses the oedipal situation to exemplify it. He writes of identification as

---

1. For two recent expositions of this view from a philosophical perspective, see Lear (1998) and Cavell (1998).

the earliest expression of an emotional tie with another person. It plays a part in the early history of the Oedipus complex. A little boy will exhibit a special interest in his father; he would like to grow like him and be like him, and take his place everywhere. We may simply say that he takes his father as an ideal. This behaviour has nothing to do with a passive or feminine attitude towards his father (and towards males in general); it is on the contrary typically masculine. It fits in well with the Oedipus complex, for which it helps prepare the way [p. 105].

According to Freud, in addition to this early identification with the father, the little boy also forms a different type of object tie to his mother:

a true object-cathexis . . . according to the attachment [anaclitic] type. [The boy] exhibits, therefore, two psychologically distinct ties: a straightforward sexual object-cathexis towards his mother and an identification with his father which takes him as his model. The two subsist side by side for a time without any mutual influence or interference. In consequence of the irresistible advance towards a unification of mental life, they come together at last; and the normal Oedipus conflict originates from their confluence. The little boy notices that his father stands in his way with his mother [p. 105].

This perception, according to Freud, leads the boy to undergo a second type of identification with the father: "His identification with his father then takes on a hostile colouring and becomes identical with the wish to replace his father in regard to his mother as well" (p. 105).

At first glance, it might seem that there is little difference between the two types of identification other than that the former is friendly, while the latter is rivalrous and hostile. But closer inspection reveals a more important difference. The boy's wish to be like the father is a far more sophisticated psychological achievement than his wish to replace the father. His wish to be like the father is an aspiration, which means that it is necessarily coupled with the awareness that he is not the father (otherwise it would not be necessary for the boy to wish to be like him; one need not wish to be what one believes one already is). The boy who wishes to replace his father is like a passenger on an airliner who, despite being unable to pilot an airplane, wants to replace the pilot with himself. The belief that this would be safe or sane is quite different from, say, admiring the pilot and wishing someday to be a pilot, as an aspiration. It implies that the boy believes he already *is* like his father, and is therefore *able* to replace him.

While this belief is, like the more affectionate identification, clearly the product of a wish, it is, unlike the more affectionate identification, the product of a wish that is felt to have been magically fulfilled. It takes no account at all of the realistic difficulties that a small boy would have actually filling his father's shoes.

The boy's belief that he *is* the father is an omnipotent identification: it is based on the idea that what the boy *aspires* to be, he already is. In other words, it is the expression of an omnipotent fantasy, a fantasy that is felt to be a reality. Such identifications act as defenses against the awareness of the differences between the boy and his father. Insofar as they are successful, they undermine the father's status as an object for the boy—as someone who differs from him—and also undermine the part of the boy's subjectivity or ego that takes the father as an object. The boy's wish to be *like* the father, on the other hand, implies a realistic awareness that he is *not* the father. It is not an omnipotent identification, like the belief that he is the father, because it does not equate the boy with his father—it does not eliminate the difference between self and object. To distinguish this from the type of identification that eliminates subject and object by equating the two, I call it an aspiration.

Omnipotent identifications tend to produce difficulties in distinguishing self from object, whereas aspiration preserves both the object as an object and the subject as a subject, since the subject is not equating itself with the object. Aspirations are fundamentally respectful of the differences between self and object.[2]

The oedipal conflict is not primarily a conflict *between* the boy and his father with his mother as the prize, although it may play itself out that way. It is, first of all, an intrapsychic conflict, a conflict *within* the boy

---

2. For a fuller exposition of the two phenomena, see Caper (1999, chapter 9). Freud (1939) was still trying to straighten out the chronology of these two types of identification many years later, when he wrote the following notes: "'Having' and 'being' in children. Children like expressing an object-relation by an identification: 'I am the object.' 'Having' is the later of the two. After the loss of the object it relapses into being. Example: the breast. 'The breast is part of me, I am the breast.' Only later: 'I have it'—that is, 'I am not it'" (p. 299).

between his love for his father as model or ideal to which he aspires—his having his father as an object—and his elimination of his father as an object through identification with him. The oedipal conflict, whatever else it might be, is a conflict between the boy's capacity to have his father as an object and his need to *be* the father through omnipotent identification with him.

The outcome of the Oedipus complex—the type of superego that emerges from it—depends on what unconscious choice is made between these two types of links to the father. If omnipotent identification predominates, the outcome is pathological and the superego that emerges from the oedipal resolution is harsh, omnipotent, and archaic. If a relationship with the father as an object separate from himself predominates, the superego that emerges in the boy will be more benign, realistic, and mature.

Another way of putting this would be to say that identification tends to eliminate the father as an object, and therefore the boy as a subject vis-à-vis the father, which impoverishes his subjectivity or ego, whereas aspiration tends to preserve the father as an object distinct from the boy and also the boy's subjectivity as a subject distinct from the father; in other words, aspiration strengthens his ego.

Freud discussed identification in his book on group psychology at such length because he considered the identification of the members of a group with one another to be the glue that held the group together. He divided groups into two distinct types. One he called "unorganized" or "spontaneous" and the other, "organized" (with the implication that organized groups do not form spontaneously, i.e., that their formation requires work). Examples of organized groups are the social groups responsible for the many cultural achievements that would not be possible without the activity of a group (visual arts, science, music, performing arts, and language itself, to name a few). The prime example of unorganized or spontaneous groups is a mob. (Freud based his study of such groups on Le Bon's analysis of the mobs that roamed Paris during the Terror.)

Following McDougall (1920), Freud (1921) stipulates that an "organized" group possesses the following characteristics: it has some continuity of existence; the individuals in the group have "some definite idea . . . of the nature, composition, functions and capacities of the group" (p. 86); it interacts with other groups similar to it but differing from it in many respects; it possesses traditions, customs, and habits; and, finally, it has a definite structure, expressed in the specialization and differentiation of the function of its members. He then comments that

> it seems to us that the condition which McDougall designates as the "organization" of a group can with more justification be described in another way. The problem consists in how to procure for the group precisely those features which were characteristic of the individual and which were extinguished in him by the formation of the group. For the individual, outside the primitive group, possessed his own continuity, his self-consciousness, his traditions and customs, his own particular function and position, and he kept apart from his rivals. Owing to his entry into an "unorganized" group, he had lost this distinctiveness for a time [pp. 86–87].

It is important to note that when Freud says that features "characteristic of the individual [are] extinguished in him by the formation of the group," he is referring not to all groups, but only to "unorganized" groups. An individual who becomes part of an organized group does not lose those characteristics—that is, he does not lose his own identity. On the contrary, we might say, rather, that someone with a talent for art, science, or language can fully realize his identity only as part of an "organized" community of artists, scientists, and language-speakers. The conclusion we can draw, then, is that, in Freud's schema, the formation of the unorganized group is effected by the individuals' within it losing their distinctive identities; at the same time, the formation of an organized group depends on the individuals' that compose it retaining their distinctive identities.

The erasure of identity that occurs when an individual becomes part of an unorganized group is analogous to a boy's identification with his father—his unconscious belief that he really is his father and therefore can replace him, which causes him both to lose his identity as a child and his concept of his father as someone different from himself. The type of identification that occurs between members of the organized group, on the other hand, is analogous to the boy's aspiration to be *like* his father, which allows him to preserve the father as an object in his mind—as someone different from himself—and at the same time allows him to preserve his own identity or ego, his knowledge of who he really is.

PRIMITIVE AND SOPHISTICATED GROUPS

These fundamental differences in the relationship of the members of the two different types of group to each other and to their own identities was taken up 40 years after Freud's work on groups by Wilfred Bion (1961). Bion developed the concept of "basic assumption" activity. Basic assumption activity is what characterizes basic assumption groups. Basic assumption groups are dominated by powerful unconscious fantasies, and their purpose seems to consist of an attempt to validate these phantasies.

Groups whose functioning is pure expressions of basic assumption activity do not exist (since their contact with mundane reality would be too poor to allow them to survive), but some actual groups come close: mass ecstasy, mass panic, and lynch mobs come to mind as examples. But, just as no real group is completely out of touch with mundane reality, no group is completely devoid of basic assumption activity. Such a group, were it to exist, would lack the emotional vitality needed to survive as a human group: it would lack the fundamental emotional protoforces that give rise to dreams, wishes, desires, and aspirations. In *all* groups, basic assumption activity exists mixed in with realistic activity, in the same way that yellow and blue exist in all green things. But we need a prism to see the yellow and blue. Bion's theory of groups is the prism that allows us to distinguish basic assumption activity from other psychological activities of the group.

To illustrate what I mean, one type of basic assumption activity, which Bion called the dependent mentality, is dominated by the unconscious fantasy that the group's leader will (sooner or later) solve all the problems facing the group. No real work on the problems facing the group is necessary, and in fact the suggestion that realistic work on those problems might be a good idea, just in case, is considered blasphemous, since it implies that the leader's powers are so limited that they might actually need some assistance from mundane effort. Bion used an example from Freud's paper on groups, the Church, as an illustration of the dependent type of basic assumption group.

A second type of basic assumption activity is what Bion called fight–flight activity, the defining fantasy of which is that all of the group's problems lie outside it and that the leader's job is therefore to arm the group to do battle with these external enemies and thus protect the goodness of the group from external threat. Bion's example of such a group, also taken from Freud, was the Army.

If my description of these basic assumptions has made them sound unreasonable, that is because they are. But it is important to keep in mind that a group that was completely reasonable would not be a human group—it would lack the emotional vitality that makes groups human. All actual groups are therefore complex combinations of basic assumption mentality and what Bion called work group mentality, which is far more realistic. These include the Army and the Church, as well as every other social activity or institution, psychoanalysis not excepted. I will return to this point later, but for now I wish to focus on the basic assumption mentality of these groups.

The members of a basic assumption group experience an emotional ambiance that is intense, close, and characterized by a sense of purpose and direction that is felt to be sacred. This ambience is exclusive: any member of the group who fails to support and partake in it is expelled from the group. He becomes a pariah, like an atheist at a Church Synod or a diplomat at a military General Staff meeting. Bion's basic assumption groups correspond quite closely to Freud's "unorganized" groups, but his view of them makes it clear, in a way that Freud's does not, that such groups are by no means really unorganized. They are highly organized in support of specific unconscious beliefs. That the members of such groups form highly complex organizations dedicated to isolating their basic assumption beliefs from reasoned assessment implies that the members of these groups fear that the conjunction of these beliefs with reason would destroy either the emotional forces they embody or reason itself. A constructive conjunction with reason seems to be beyond the scope of the basic assumption group's imagination. I shall elaborate on this point at the end of this chapter.

Bion also described a quite different type of group that he called a work group. Work groups correspond roughly to Freud's "organized" groups and are characterized by their recognition of their own limitations in solving the problems facing the group, by a sense of the boundaries of the group, and by a sense of the distinctions among the individuals of which the group is composed. Work groups have a more or less well-defined task and a realistic approach to discharging it. In brief, work groups are the products of definition and distinction: between themselves and the outside world, between what they wish to do and what they can do, among the distinct individuals composing them, and between the task they are charged with and all other tasks. I have labeled as primitive groups those which follow the pattern of Freud's "unorganized" groups and Bion's basic assumption groups; and those which follow the pattern of Freud's "organized" groups and Bion's work groups, I have called sophisticated groups.

PRIMITIVE AND SOPHISTICATED PSYCHOANALYTIC GROUPS

Bion suggested that the psychoanalyst and his patient—the psychoanalytic dyad—may itself be regarded as a group of two. I propose that it is at one and the same time a primitive and a sophisticated type of group. Psychoanalyst and patient are simultaneously linked by identifications with each other that eliminate their separate identities and by other links that recognize and preserve their separate identities.

In the sophisticated group, patient and analyst cooperate with one another as individuals engaged in a joint task. Cooperation on a task includes conflict and disagreement, and individuals engaging in a cooperative endeavor are just that—individuals—who retain their own identities and points of view while cooperating and conflicting with each other.

In the primitive group, there is no real cooperation or conflict, but instead a kind of mutual identification of the individuals involved to produce the emotional ambiance associated with basic assumption groups, which is at once tenuous and tenacious. This mutual identification tends to eliminate from the life of the group any emotion not supporting the assumptions that maintain the group's emotional ambiance.

Once we see the distinction between the analyst–patient dyad as a homogeneous group of two and the analyst and patient as cooperating individuals, it becomes possible to see that one of the tasks that analyst and patient are cooperating on as distinct individuals is the investigation of themselves engaging in mutual identification. (Mutual identification, while it occurs in every analysis, is not, of course, the same as empathy, in which one identifies with the state of mind of one's object *without* losing any part of one's own identity.) Part of the task of the sophisticated (working) patient–analyst dyad is precisely the reflexive examination of the primitive patient–analyst dyad, and part of the task of the primitive patient–analyst dyad is to subject itself to this examination. The task of each in an analysis is to enter into some kind of marriage with the other: the primitive group must allow itself to be examined by the sophisticated one, and the sophisticated group must examine the primitive group without attempting to do anything other than examine it, such as alter or "correct" it. In other words, each must respect the needs of the other.

Since the sophisticated work of analysis is a cooperative investigation, it can occur only in an atmosphere in which cooperation is possible, and cooperation between individuals is possible only where there are distinct individuals. But it is precisely individual distinctiveness that is lost in the primitive dyad. There is thus in every analysis an irresolvable and perennial conflict or tension between the primitive patient–analyst dyad and the sophisticated patient–analyst dyad. This tension may perhaps be best understood by noting that in analysis, the primitive and sophisticated dyads form at the expense of each other. It is important to emphasize, however, that, since the work of the sophisticated (working) patient–analyst dyad is the examination of the primitive patient–analyst dyad, *both* are necessary for a working analysis to take place, and neither one may be permitted to extinguish the other.

The primitive group acts at all times to support its own basic assumptions. These are expressed in analysis as preconceptions about what analysis is or should be and what the link between patient and analyst is or should be. Since these basic assumptions are felt a priori to be vital to the emotional survival of the analysis, they must remain unexposed to the actual experiences of patient and analyst lest they come to be felt to be untrue. (This does not mean that they will not, in fact, withstand exposure to the actual experience of patient and analyst. It means merely that the basic assumption group believes it will not withstand such exposure.) The sophisticated patient–analyst dyad examines the assumptions of the primitive dyad in the light of the actual experiences of the two individuals involved.

The reflexive nature of the psychoanalytic work requires both the primitive and the sophisticated dyads to remain vital and to remain in contact with one another. The clinical sign of this contact is a tension between the two dyads that is experienced by both patient and analyst as a sense of insecurity in the analysis.

CLINICAL ILLUSTRATION

The following example of how the primitive psychoanalytic group manifests itself clinically describes a phenomenon that I think will be familiar to most analysts. It is the tendency of patients to feel at certain times that the analyst is being artificial when he is practicing the rule of analytic abstinence, that is, when he is abstaining from having with the patient the kind of social relationship he has with his friends and family. The patient may express this feeling as a wish for what he calls a more real relationship with the analyst, which often turns out to mean that he wishes the analyst to enact the role of one or another of the patient's transference figures. The figure that the patient wants the analyst to simulate may be friendly or hostile, warm or cold, reassuring or alarming, sadistic or masochistic, but what it never is, is an analyst. If the analyst persists in just doing analysis when the patient is under the influence of this wish, the patient may come to feel that the analyst is stuck in an artificial stance, not telling the patient what he "really" thinks about him, and that if he would only speak more spontaneously, then the analysis would become more "real." "Spontaneous" in this context almost always turns out to mean less thoughtful, reflective, and analytic.

The patient's feeling that the analyst is being artificial is never a feeling that the analyst is being properly artificial, that is, adopting certain technical rules of behavior so he may practice the art of psychoanalysis. It is a feeling that the analyst is doing something wrong, something unreal, something he should not be doing, and that, if the analyst would just stop doing it, the analysis would progress. This feeling is fervently expressed by patients who would be horrified at the thought of, say, their surgeon or internist, or even their accountant, being less than careful, thoughtful, and circumspect when they were working.

James Strachey (1934) touched on this problem:

[T]he analytic situation is all the time threatening to degenerate into a "real" situation. But this actually means the opposite of what it appears to. It means that the patient is all the time on the brink of turning the real external object (the analyst) into the archaic one; that is to say, he is on the brink of projecting his primitive introjected imagos on to him. In so far as the patient actually does this, the analyst becomes like anyone else that he meets in real life—a phantasy object [p. 284].

What Strachey means here is that the internal objects that the patient is under pressure to project into the analyst—and puts the analyst under pressure to enact—tend to be quite fantastic. He goes on to say that, insofar as the patient succeeds in regarding the analyst as a phantasy object,

> [t]he analyst then ceases to possess the peculiar advantages derived from the analytic situation; he will be introjected like all other phantasy objects into the patient's superego, and will no longer be able to function in the peculiar ways which are essential to [his being an analyst]. In this difficulty the patient's sense of reality is an essential but a very feeble ally; indeed, an improvement in it is one of the things that we hope the analysis will bring about. It is important, therefore, not to submit it to any unnecessary strain.

The strain that Strachey refers to is the analyst's acting like the patient's archaic object, which strains the patient's ability to see the analyst for what he really is—an analyst. Strachey goes on

> that is the fundamental reason why the analyst must avoid any real behaviour that is likely to confirm the patient's view of him as a "bad" or a "good" phantasy object. This is perhaps more obvious as regards the "bad" object. If, for instance, the analyst were to show that he was really shocked or frightened by one of the patient's id-impulses, the patient would immediately treat him in that respect as a dangerous object and introject him into his archaic severe superego. . . . [But it] may be equally unwise for the analyst to act really in such a way as to encourage the patient to project his "good" introjected object on to him. For the patient will then tend to regard him as a good object in an archaic sense and will incorporate him with his archaic "good" imagos and will use him as a protection against his "bad" ones. In that way, his infantile positive impulses as well as his negative ones may escape analysis, for there may no

longer be a possibility for his ego to make a comparison between the phantasy external object and the real one. It will perhaps be argued that, with the best will in the world, the analyst, however careful he may be, will be unable to prevent the patient from projecting these various imagos on to him. This is of course indisputable, and indeed, the whole effectiveness of analysis depends upon its being so. The lesson of these difficulties is merely to remind us that the patient's sense of reality has the narrowest limits [pp. 284–285].

Now, of course, when Strachey writes that the "the patient's sense of reality has the narrowest limits," he is not talking just about psychotic patients. He is referring to the fact that the reality sense of even nonpsychotic patients becomes impaired in the heat of the activities of the primitive psychoanalytic dyad.

One aspect of this problem is that there is a very powerful tendency, as a result of his projection of his archaic superego into the analyst, for the patient to actively monitor the analyst's interpretations for evidence of love or hatred, approval or disapproval, instead of taking them as observations about the patient's state of mind. The patient is listening for whether the analyst thinks he is good or bad, lovable or disgusting, pathetic, terrifying. He is always asking himself, "Does he [the analyst] think what I've said is good, or does he think it's bad?" This concern with whether the analyst's interpretations are expressions of love or hatred of the patient has nothing to do with what the analyst is *trying* to do with his interpretations, which is simply to observe something about the patient and to describe it to him in a scientific way (for want of a better term)—that is, in such a way that the patient is able simply to think about it as an observation, not as an expression of approval or disapproval.[3]

---

3. I have suggested elsewhere (Caper, 1999, chapter 2) that what Strachey calls the analyst's function as an "auxiliary superego" should really be called an "auxiliary ego," since the analyst is concerned only with what is, in Strachey's words, "real and contemporary" about the patient, and not with whether it is good or bad, and wants only to communicate his observation about the patient without fear or favor.

This is what we try to do as analysts, but not, in fact, what we actually end up doing, at least not all the time, because, when we try to do just this, we find that it is very difficult. We find ourselves subject to all kinds of subtle or not-so-subtle psychological pressures, emanating from the patient and from ourselves, to do something else instead—that is, to enact the role of the archaic internal object that the patient has projected into us. For example, we may find ourselves provoked by the patient and find ourselves at least wanting to make an "interpretation" that will sting, and sometimes, it must be confessed, we do that, instead of doing what we should be doing, which is figuring out (through self-analysis) what is making us so angry and using that as the basis of a more properly analytic interpretation. At other times, we find ourselves not so much angry at the patient as afraid of him, and then we find ourselves wanting to make an "interpretation" that will reassure or soothe him. Here, too, we must confess that we find ourselves doing that, instead of similarly analyzing in ourselves *why* we want to make the patient feel good (or at least better) and using that as the basis for an interpretation. The same goes for our finding ourselves infatuated with a patient and making interpretations that are seductive. (For a more detailed discussion of this point, see Caper, 1999, chapter 2.) Such "interpretations," made without benefit of self-analysis, are thoughtless in the strict sense of the word: they are not products of the analyst's thoughtful consideration of his countertransference love or hatred; they are simply products of his countertransference. The problem with unconsidered countertransference, of course, is that we find ourselves behaving in the manner to which the patient has provoked or seduced us, which means we are behaving like what the patient calls his "real" objects (meaning the objects in his "real" life, his life outside analysis), whom he also provokes and seduces in the course of perpetuating his neurotic object relationships.

But this object that is so "real" from the patient's point of view is precisely the external fantasy object that Strachey describes. If the analyst behaves in a way that is congruent with the archaic internal object that the patient is projecting into him, his behavior will, as Strachey pointed out, deprive the patient of the opportunity to compare and contrast his internal object with the external one—the analyst. And this will in turn deprive him of the chance to differentiate his fantasies from reality, or what is himself—internal reality—from what is his object—external reality. The paradox here is that what the patient may insist is the analyst's "being real" is precisely what is best calculated to undermine the patient's sense of reality, or, what in my view is more or less the same thing, his capacity to distinguish internal from external reality.

What the patient sometimes calls a real relationship with the analyst is therefore a way of talking about the analyst's acting in a way that is congruent with an unconscious fantasy of the patient's and demonstrating by his words and demeanor his unquestioning emotional commitment to doing so. In this way, the patient and analyst form a primitive group dominated by devotion to the basic assumption fantasy it exists to serve. The analyst is under pressure to conform to the patient's unconscious fantasies of what he should be like under pain of emotional expulsion from the analytic dyad.

But for the analytic dyad to become a primitive one, more is required than the patient's psychological pressure on the analyst to revere and embody his unconscious basic assumptions. A primitive group consists of individuals who are *all* in the grip of the same basic assumption belief. For the analytic dyad to manifest true primitive mentality, the analyst must (for reasons of his own) have unconscious wishes for the patient that are congruent with the patient's unconscious wishes for the analyst. For example, the patient may wish the analyst to be a magical healer, and the analyst may unconsciously welcome this view of himself. Unless the analyst is able to analyze this belief, he will unconsciously pressure the patient to act in a way that is congruent with it.

If the analyst's pressure on the patient is congruent with the patient's pressure on the analyst, that is, if they are both dominated by the same basic assumption fantasy, then the pressure for enactment will not seem like pressure to either one; instead, both will feel that they are engaging in a "real" relationship that transcends the stodgy technical rules of analysis. The fantastic nature of this real relationship cannot be examined in this situation, since there is no one who is able even seriously to imagine that it is a fantasy. The nonanalytic nature of the relationship may be recognized, but in this case it will be viewed not as nonanalytic, but rather as merely nontraditional, and rationalized as an innovative development in analytic technique.

A psychological regression to a primitive group will thus become rationalized, under the force of the gratification that such a regression provides, as progress in psychoanalysis.

DISCUSSION

Primitive Group Mentality, the Archaic Superego, and Learning From Experience

Basic assumption groups are characterized by a kind of likemindedness between the members of the group that displaces what would otherwise be thoughtful contact between distinct and differentiated individuals. What is sometimes called the real relationship in analysis, to the extent that it differs from the patient and analyst's cooperating to explore the patient's unconscious, may be no more than a psychological fusion between two individuals effected through a mutual identification around a common fantasy—an unconscious *folie à deux*. One believes in this fantasy not because of the evidence for it, but because of the rewarding sensation—the warm, close, intense, special, but somehow tenuous emotional ambiance—that corresponds to the feelings that one gets when conforming to the dictates of an archaic superego, and the persecuting pangs that correspond to the feelings that one gets when one is not conforming to them. The primitive group, including the primitive psychoanalytic dyad, is based on a kind of mutual identification that ensures that certain fantasies or beliefs remain sacred—that is, are not investigated or inquired into.

The resemblance of the emotional constellation that characterizes such a group to states of mind dominated by an archaic superego suggests that the archaic superego may be viewed as the intrapsychic representative of the primitive group—that is, as the product of a type of identification with one's objects that eliminates both object as object and subject as subject. In this type of identification, a link between subject and object is replaced by a fusion of subject and object. While this type of identification gives a verisimilitude to unconscious fantasies that produce feelings of security and warmth, it also produces an internal object—the archaic superego—from which the ego is not able to stand apart and which persecutes the ego out of exercising its functions of discriminating internal and external reality and of examining the validity of certain beliefs. If the archaic superego is indeed an intrapsychic representative of the primitive group, then the study of primitive and sophisticated groups, and particularly of the identifications that underpin them, may shed light on the nature of the archaic superego.

In the primitive psychoanalytic group, the patient wants the analyst as an external object to correspond to his internal objects (or, what is equivalent, to turn the analyst into an external fantasy object), whereas the analyst wants the patient as an object to correspond to *his* internal objects (or, what is equivalent, to turn the patient into *his* external fantasy object). But the analyst need not enact his wish for the patient; it is sufficient for him to play a merely passive role. What I mean by this is that, if there is any possibility of the analyst's words being taken as support for the patient's basic assumption fantasy, they will be, if not immediately then by the next day. Thus the analyst must actively depart from the predominant delusion—that is, he must identify and interpret it—if he is not to become part of it.

I believe that this is one of the reasons why working through is necessary in analysis, and why it is hard work for the analyst as well as the patient. What appears to be the "same" interpretation has to be given over and over because it is really not exactly the same interpretation given repeatedly; rather, it is a progressive refinement or honing of the same interpretation as it is occasioned in different contexts so that it becomes more and more difficult for the patient to assume that the analyst is participating, somehow or somewhere, in the primitive group. The analyst must also work each time to extricate himself from the gratifying basic assumption mentality into which he has drifted since the last interpretation. The effect of working through is gradually to disrupt the primitive group that is established by the congruent interaction of the analyst's unexamined assumptions and the patient's unexamined assumptions.

If the analyst cannot do this, the patient's archaic superego will be strengthened at the expense of his ego. If, on the other hand, the analyst interprets the confusion that the patient is trying to bring about, and the underlying anxieties that drive him to do it, the analyst will have strengthened the patient's ego at the expense of his archaic superego.

The approach of the primitive group to reality may be summarized as an attempt to give a semblance of reality to certain beliefs. To the extent that this attempt is successful, the members of the primitive group are able to support each other's belief that their shared fantasies are realities. In a working analysis, it is the analyst's role to support these beliefs only in a provisional and passive way, not as the result of coercion, seduction, or the gratification of his own needs, but only to see what it is that he is supposed to be in the transference so he may analyze it. Here analyzing it means helping the patient to see that what belongs to his internal world is in his internal world and that what belongs to his external world is in his external world. This activity consists precisely of the reflexive investigation of the primitive group of which he and the patient are a part, and the psychoanalyst's engaging in it makes him a unique object and psychoanalysis a unique relationship. The patient, of course, also participates in the reflexive work.

The primitive group attempts to mold perception so that certain beliefs that it feels vital to its survival may be maintained, while the sophisticated group threatens the sense of emotional security thus gained by subjecting these beliefs to the cold, harsh light of reality. Both types of mental activity are present, and must be present, in varying proportions from the beginning of the analysis onward (and, perhaps also, as I have argued [Caper, 1999, chapter 7], from the beginning of life onward).

PSYCHOANALYSIS AS A SPECIALIZED WORK GROUP

Before concluding, I would like to return to Bion's (1961) concept of the basic assumption group, and what it implies both for clinical psychoanalysis and for psychoanalysis as a cultural institution. Basic assumption activity is an abstraction. There is no such thing as a basic assumption group in pure form. All basic assumption activity must be combined with more realistic activity—what Bion called work activity—if the group within which the basic assumption activity exists is to survive. For example, the Church must aver the omnipotence of God and the efficacy of prayer; but it must also recognize that, if the members of the Church did nothing other than practice these beliefs, they would starve to death. And the Army must assert that, when push comes to shove, sufficient violence will always cut through a difficult problem; but if it did not recognize that, on occasion, something other than violence is called for, it would quickly decimate itself through endless warfare. This coexistence of basic assumption activity with attention to the demands of external reality—a blending of the two in such a way that reality does not supervene over the active basic assumption, and the active basic assumption does not entirely displace reality testing—is what Bion called a Specialized Work Group.

The job of a Specialized Work Group is to provide a safe haven for a specific basic assumption activity so that the members of the group can satisfy the emotional needs that the basic assumption activity expresses while still surviving, still meeting the demands of reality. It may be that every human institution that is both productive and emotionally significant—that is, every human institution—is a Specialized Work Group: a combination of basic assumption activity, which provides the group with emotional vitality, and work activity, which permits it to survive in the face of reality. This rule includes psychoanalysis—both the analyst's activity with a patient and his participation in psychoanalytic institutions—as a human endeavor.

As we have seen, a primitive group acts to ensure the survival of certain basic assumption beliefs that it feels are essential to the human emotional life of the group. But these beliefs do not constitute real emotion. The members of the primitive group do not feel real emotionality—the passion of real love or hatred—toward one another, because such emotions can be felt fully only by a subject that experiences itself as distinct from the object, toward an object that it feels to be distinct from itself. Instead of real emotionality toward an object, the members of the primitive group experience a sort of emotional merger with one another, the emotional tone of which is usually warm (and on occasion hot), but seldom sharp; the psychological fusion of the primitive group's members with one another has deprived each of them of the others as distinct objects, and therefore all of them of their subjectivity vis-à-vis the others. The basic assumption fantasies of the primitive group contain the seeds of passion and emotionality, but they quench real desire almost as soon as it arises, by producing the feeling that what is desired (or rather would be, if it were not already regarded as a fait accompli) is already a fact. The emotionality of a basic assumption fantasy by itself is like a two-dimensional house, which one simultaneously enters by the front door and leaves by the rear.

For real emotionality, passion, or desire to be experienced, something more than a mutual identification between members of a group (such as the psychoanalytic dyad) is clearly necessary. The basic assumption fantasy must be brought into juxtaposition with the reality that the members of the group are not identical, and specifically not identical in ways the basic assumption fantasy requires them to be. Only this juxtaposition brings the seeds of emotionality—the wish expressed in the basic assumption fantasy—into conjunction with the opportunity for this protoemotionality to be realized and live emotion to be experienced.[4] This opportunity consists precisely of the awareness that subject and object are not fused, which permits the subject to experience itself as a subject, the object as a distinct object, and the distinct emotional link between the two as a link, not a fusion.

To illustrate what I mean, we may take love and hatred as examples of emotionality: to experience love and hatred in their fully developed forms, one must be able to tolerate what one feels. But for this to occur, one must be able to distinguish what one feels from what others feel. It is precisely this sense of one's emotionality, distinct from that of others, that is missing in the basic assumption group. The conjunction of the primitive group with the sophisticated group permits love and hatred to be experienced in a fully developed way, because it permits the experience of a distinct self, aware of its love or hatred, as well as the experience of a distinct object—a who or what, different from the self, toward which one feels love or hatred. Knowing what one loves or hates—and feels in general—implies contact with one's emotionality and with some clear picture of an object. Without such contact between a distinct self and a distinct object, live emotion cannot be experienced.

The task of the working psychoanalytic dyad is to make room for its protoemotionality, the emotionality contained within the primitive dyad's basic assumption fantasies, but not experienced as live emotion by either member of the dyad. This is sometimes referred to as containment of primitive emotional forces by the analysis, but containment must be understood here in a specific way. It does not mean control or restriction. It does not mean trimming primitive emotional needs so they fit into a sophisticated (rational) picture of the mental life of the group (or dyad). It means encompassing primitive protoemotions in a way that, far from controlling them, permits their realization as fully formed emotion. A classic example of such a process is an interpretation that brings an emotion that has been split off or repressed (perhaps precisely because it is felt to be too "primitive") into consciousness, where it and its ramifications may be more fully experienced.

The task of the working psychoanalytic dyad is to weave the latent emotionality of the primitive group into a context—to determine in what

---

4. I am distinguishing here live emotionality from the torpid fusion of mutual identification.

sense the emotionality makes sense. This is the same as determining what the emotionality means. In this way, the latent emotionality of the basic assumption group gains expression, becomes experiential, and becomes part of the mind—that is, part of a true object relationship, instead of a fusion that is essentially torpid, however warm its ambiance.

While knowing what or who one loves and hates makes one more real, this knowledge also constrains one. We can no longer believe whatever is most comfortable or convenient to believe about ourselves but must believe what we have come to know. As Freud justly remarked, psychoanalysis has disturbed the sleep of the world. This process often involves a great deal of suffering, both in the modern sense of painful experience and in the older sense of patience and tolerance.

Clinical psychoanalysis, the work between one patient and one analyst, is a very peculiar Specialized Work Group. Its work consists of the unique reflexive task of thinking about its own basic assumption activity. This work is highly creative, in the sense that it allows the primitive group's protoemotions (the only type of emotionality possible in the primitive group's more or less objectless state) to become actually experienced emotion and also allows the sophisticated, reasonable group to be vitalized by an emotionality that it would lack without contact with the primitive group.

But this work is accompanied by a great sense of insecurity, because the conjunction of primitive and sophisticated forces seems to be accompanied regularly by the fear that each will destroy the other. The analytic pair feels that this examination of basic assumptions threatens it either with the sophisticated group's being overwhelmed by the primitive one, with a consequent burst of uncontrollable feeling, or with the primitive group's being overwhelmed by the sophisticated one, with a consequent extinction of feeling.

And here again we encounter Oedipus: the creative union between primitive and sophisticated activity that is hoped for in analysis and the destructive union that is feared are two versions of the primal scene. The questions always present in any psychoanalysis are, is creative "sexual" union between these two different types of force possible, and is destructive union between them avoidable? This uncertainty produces the insecurity inherent in psychoanalysis.

Psychoanalysis, whose work it is to bring together the primitive and sophisticated groups, cannot, unlike the Church or the Army, provide the kind of permanent, safe emotional haven of the unexamined basic assumption group, with its never-quite-experienced and never-quite-extinguished emotionality. A working analysis is carried out in an atmosphere that is tense and insecure, precisely because it aims ultimately to examine basic assumptions, which brings them into conjunction with the sophisticated group in a way that threatens the extinction either of primitive emotionality or sophisticated realism. The emotional security brought about by analysis consists only in what may be obtained from knowing what one's fantasies are, without regard to the possibility of their being satisfied, and from knowing what is a fantasy and what is not.

If this kind of security sounds like a small reward for undergoing the rigors of analysis, we need to remind ourselves that the development I am describing is what is commonly referred to as sanity and that the security that is gained from having access to it is hardly insignificant. But it is sanity purchased at the price of the kind of security obtained from splitting apart the primitive and sophisticated groups, a split that keeps both the emotionality of the primitive group tepid and diffuse and the rationality of the sophisticated group reasonable.

As a cultural institution—the group of all analysts working together—psychoanalysis has taken upon itself the same uniquely reflexive task of examining its own basic assumptions. This is a revolutionary attitude toward such fundamental emotional protoforces. But revolutions produce counterrevolutions, and one of the ways in which basic assumption activity reasserts itself in psychoanalysis is in a movement back from psychoanalytic work—from an examination of the basic assumption activity of the analytic group of two in the light of reason and experience—to a reliance on either split-off basic assumption activity or split-off sophisticated activity. From work focused on trying to obtain an objective picture of our emotional basic assumption beliefs and a full experience of the emotion contained in them, we tend to settle back either into an uncritical acceptance of those beliefs, or into a pseudo-reasonable explaining-away of them as "irrational." Both possibilities result in a blunting of live emotional experience *and a consequent loss of the senses of internal and external reality, both of which depend on an accurate and precise apprehension of emotional experience.*

The pseudo-reasonable explaining-away of "irrational" beliefs makes its appearance in clinical psychoanalysis as an attempt to label certain emotional experiences as "primitive," "infantile," or "pathological," as a way of suppressing or dismissing them. This is the so-called authoritarian analysis.

The uncritical acceptance of basic assumption beliefs is a reaction to this and is a recent type of reversion from radical analytic integration of primitive and sophisticated activities. It is the idea of the so-called good analytic relationship—the idea that, if the two participants can only maintain an agreeable enough relationship between themselves, then resistance will slowly evaporate under the impact of its warmth and trust, and insight will arise in its place. This idea is quite different from the notion that interpretation and the laborious working through of resistances are what *make* a good analytic relationship. In other words, the analytic relationship is what it is, and uniquely what it is, because it is an *interpreted* relationship, a state of affairs that two people have had to work very hard to achieve, and will have to work very hard to maintain, and one that both of them, as much as they want to achieve and maintain it, also do not want.

The difference between these two types of relationships is the difference between, on one hand, a good relationship that is cultivated by patient and analyst by encouraging the feeling that it is good (and rooting out the opposite), and, on the other, a good relationship that is felt to be good because of the experience that it can work productively and meet the challenges of the relationship (including the bad aspects of the relationship) realistically.[5]

The current controversy in this area dates back to only a few years after Freud wrote *Group Psychology,* to the *Symposium on Child Analysis* (Klein, 1927), in which Melanie Klein argued against Anna Freud's contention that the analyst should instill in the child a sense of security so that the child will trust her enough to accept her interpretations. Klein argued that interpretation must come first, since it is this that produces real trust, trust based on a realistic appreciation that the analyst is in a universe different from that of the archaic superego.

This stance requires considerable courage and faith in analysis on the part of the analyst, and its essence was well expressed by Klein:

[W]hat we have to do with children as well as with adults is not simply to establish and maintain the analytic situation by every analytic means and refrain from all *direct* educative influence, but,

---

5. Much the same can be said of any human relationship, but that discussion is beyond the scope of this paper.

more than that, a children's analyst must have the same unconscious attitude as we require in the analyst of adults, if he is to be successful. It must enable him to be really willing *only to analyze* and not to wish to mold and direct the minds of his patients. If anxiety does not prevent him, he will be able calmly to wait for the development of the correct issue, and in this way that issue will be achieved [p. 167].

PSYCHOANALYSIS AS A PAIRING GROUP

Bion (1961) described a third type of basic assumption group, which, unlike the other two, does not correspond to either of the two examples of "unorganized" group activity mentioned by Freud. Bion called this type of basic assumption activity the "pairing group." That the psychoanalytic dyad consists of a pair of people immediately raises the question of what role, if any, the pairing basic assumption plays in the psychoanalytic process.

According to Bion, the pairing group is characterized by a feeling of hope, a feeling that is

at the opposite pole to feelings of hatred, destructiveness and despair. For the feelings of hope to be sustained it is essential that the "leader" of the group, unlike the leader of the dependent group and of the fight–flight group, should be unborn. It is a person or idea that will save the group—in fact from feelings of hatred, destructiveness, and despair, of its own or of another group—but in order to do this, obviously, the Messianic hope must never be fulfilled. . . . [under the influence of the pairing basic assumption] there is a tendency for the work group to be influenced in the direction of producing a Messiah, be it person, idea, or Utopia. In so far as it succeeds, hope is weakened; for obviously nothing is then to hope for, and, since destructiveness, hatred, and despair have in no way been radically influenced, their existence again makes itself felt. This in turn accelerates a further weakening of hope. Therefore, the members of the pairing group] should see to it that Messianic hopes do not materialize [pp. 151–152].

It is tempting to suppose that one of the ways that the pairing basic assumption mentality manifests itself in psychoanalysis is through a fantasy, which may be the patient's, the analyst's, or both, that the analysis will someday, somehow release them from the inescapable tension between the primitive and sophisticated dyads that I have suggested is inherent in psychoanalysis itself. This tension, we recall, arises from the facts that the primitive and the sophisticated groups form at the expense of each other; that hatred between them is therefore inevitable; and that, despite their hatred of each other, neither can escape the other, since the complete destruction or disappearance of either one would render analysis, which requires their juxtaposition, impossible. Hence the necessary presence of this tension in every working analysis.

And hence also the wish to escape it. The Messianic hope, the hallmark of the psychoanalytic pairing group, may then consist of the theme that the psychoanalytic pair will someday produce a result—called "having been analyzed"—that amounts to being finally released from this tension and conflict.

One variation on this theme is the idea that the unconscious will be rendered entirely conscious, that reason will replace passion, and that the patient, as a result of analysis, will simply become "reasonable." This result, of course, would amount in reality to a destruction of the unconscious and a deadening of the patient. Another variation on the theme is the idea that analysis will someday allow one to experience one's passions without conflict or frustration.

Bion suggested that the Messianic hope must always be regarded as something that lies in the future, since any present, real-time candidate for Messiah or Utopia is doomed to disappoint. But, if we regard the psychoanalytic dyad as a pairing group in the sense I have indicated, there is another reason why the Messiah must never come. The resolution of the tension and hatred between the mutually dependent primitive and sophisticated psychoanalytic groups is equivalent to the death of the analysis. In this sense, the Messianic hope corresponds to the Nirvana principle (Low, 1920, p. 73), a hypothetical state in which the goal of Freud's pleasure principle is realized through the discharge of all tension (unpleasure). But, as Freud (1920) pointed out, such a state is equivalent to death. The psychoanalytic dyad, as much as it wishes for such a Messiah, also fears it with good reason, since its arrival would amount to an annihilation of the vital tension that informs every live analysis—and every life.

REFERENCES

Bion, W. (1961), *Experiences in Groups*. New York; Basic Books.

Caper, R. (1999), *A Mind of One's Own: A Kleinian View of Self and Object*. London: New Library of Psycho-Analysis/Routledge.

Cavell, M. (1998), Triangulation, one's own mind and creativity. *Internat. J. Psycho-Anal.*, 79:449–467.

Freud, S. (1920), *Beyond the Pleasure Principle. Standard Edition*, 18:1–64. London: Hogarth Press, 1955.

Freud, S. (1921), *Group Psychology and the Analysis of the Ego. Standard Edition*, 18:69–143. London: Hogarth Press, 1955.

Freud, S. (1941), *Findings, Ideas, Problems. Standard Edition*, 23:299–300. London: Hogarth Press, 1964.

Klein, M. (1927), Symposium on child analysis. In *The Writings of Melanie Klein, Vol. 1: Love, Guilt and Reparation and Other Works, 1921–1945*. London: Hogarth Press, pp. 139–169, 1975.

Lear, J. (1998), *Open Minded: Working Out the Logic of the Soul*. Cambridge, MA: Harvard University Press.

Low, B. (1920), *Psycho-Analysis: A Brief Account of the Freudian Theory*. London: Allen & Unwin.

McDougall, W. (1920), *The Group Mind*. Cambridge, UK: Cambridge University Press.

Strachey, J. (1934), The nature of the therapeutic action of psychoanalysis. *Internat. J. Psycho-Anal.*, 15:127–159.

Power and Leadership in Complex Organizations

ABRAHAM ZALEZNIK

It is easy to pick a fight with Freud. And perhaps the easiest subject for a quarrel, at least for a sociologically oriented psychoanalyst, is Freud's (1921) *Group Psychology and the Analysis of the Ego*.

While his focus, and perhaps motivation, in writing *Group Psychology* was to show that Le Bon's mob and Trotter's herd were special cases of libido theory rather than primary instincts, the contentious questions arising from this work reflect the limited examples Freud used in his essay. The Church and the Army offered excellent examples of artificial groups with which to buttress his argument that neither suggestibility to account for mob behavior nor gregariousness for the phenomena of the herd are explanatory theories. Thus, through a detour into hypnosis, one of his favorite subjects from the early days of psychoanalysis, he arrived at the formula for group formation and cohesion: A primary group . . . is a number of individuals who have put one and the same object in the place of their ego ideal and have consequently identified themselves with one another in their ego (p. 116).

In the literature of sociology, the term primary group refers to a group with few enough members to permit face-to-face interaction. Besides the family, the exemplar of the primary group, there are spontaneous groups (Whyte, 1943), such as street corner gangs, and work groups, found in factories and offices (Zaleznik, 1956). In the Church and the Army, there are primary groups, according to the sociologist's definition. But the nature of the identifications in both these venerable and massive organizations extend far beyond the primary groups that are simply entities in these large and complex organizations. While attachment to and identification with the leader is important in the cohesion of the small group, the powerful larger identifications occur in a more abstract form. In the Church, members identify with Christ; and, in the military, with the code elaborated through history, patriotism, and the glory of ancient battles fought and won through heroism. These identifications are abstractions, given force and meaning in ritual and, in theory if not in fact, in the ties that bind the leader and the led in the primary groups. The link between the abstractions that form the foundation for identification and cohesion in the primary group is to be found in the rules of leadership governing human relations. An example of such a rule was succinctly stated by the historian Douglas Southall Freeman in his lecture on leadership delivered to the Army War College shortly after World War II: First, "know your stuff"; second, "be a man"; third, "take care of your men."

The sociologist's quarrel with Freud continues. In his urgency to assert the primacy of libido theory in group formations, Freud neglected the observation that groups, particularly in large, complex organizations, form as a result of contracts, explicit or implicit, that give expression to self-interests. Freud's distinguishing between primary and artificial groups placed him on the edge of dealing with a subject broader than the examples of the Church and the Army could possibly permit. Instead of calling large organizations artificial groups, I refer to them as complex organizations. This term will permit considering a broad range of organizations, whether business, education, public service, or political.

Freud recognized the multiplicity of groups that influence individuals, and in which identification may indeed play a significant part in the formation of the ego. Freud stated,

> Each individual is a component part of numerous groups, he is bound by ties of identification in many directions, and he has built up his ego ideal upon the various models. Each individual therefore has a share in numerous group minds—those of his race, of his class, of his creed, of his nationality, etc.—and he can also raise himself above them to the extent of having a scrap of independence and originality [p. 129].

The question Freud left open in considering the impact of the group on the individual is the extent to which being a member of a profession, including one's performance as an executive in business or in government, exerts an influence on individuals through identification or some other function of the ego. And perhaps even more challenging than the question of how a group affects individuals, is the persistent and important question of leadership, of how individuals with a "scrap of independence and originality" bring about change and enhanced economic value that accrues to the benefit of such diverse constituencies as employees and shareholders.

In acknowledging the influence of group membership on individuals, Freud also revealed his belief in the primacy of the individual over the group. Ranging from hypnosis, falling in love, and membership in groups, Freud's theory of identification was based on the principle that an individual relinquishes significant portions of potential ego autonomy in identifications and attachments, whether with single objects or group membership. The exception to this principle is found in the case of the leader. In identification, "the members of a group stand in need of the illusion that they are equally and justly loved by their leader; but the leader himself need love no one else, he may be of a masterful nature, absolutely narcissistic, self-confident and independent" (pp. 123–124). Perhaps! However, a leader may also be masterful in creating a vision, in communicating this vision to his constituents, and in negotiating conflicting opinions regarding the direction in which he seeks to move his constituents. In other words, complex organizations are not monolithic, with a single power center. However hard he may try to act out the narcissistic position, a leader has to influence his subordinates by appealing to, among other things, their interests. Thus there is a phenomenon called interest politics that applies to most complex organizations, and how a leader deals with this phenomenon becomes a variable in the display of his power and in the enactment of his leadership position. This variable may indeed involve identification, but it also involves many other ego functions, including the expression of interests and talents that flow through ego development from the earliest to the most mature years.

Many social psychologists, notably George Herbert Mead (1956), have taken exception to the conclusion that individuals become somewhat impoverished as group members and give over to the leader significant power as well as a disproportionate share of the available rewards. In contrast to Freud and psychoanalysis, Mead believed that the ego belongs to society. Socialization occurs through group memberships, starting with the family and proceeding through school, work, and voluntary organizations. Social psychologists and sociologists have grave doubts concerning the problem of narcissistic leadership. Though most often they express these doubts normatively, they believe that leaders of primary groups as well as of complex organizations aim, or rather should aim, for democratic climates in primary groups, and empowerment of subordinates in complex organizations. Leadership, in these terms, could be perceived as the conscious effort to diminish one's own power by transferring power to the group even at the expense of the designated leader's autonomy. Indeed, the narcissistic leader has no place in this ethos of group psychology so popular in America (Lewin, Lippit, and White, 1939).

There is one more important argument in this litany of how one can quarrel with Freud over his group psychology. In Freud's haste to elaborate the libido theory and the derivation of group psychology from the myth of the primal horde, in which the youngest son killed the father and gave birth to totemism in the band of brothers, Freud overlooked the phenomenon of designated authority and allied roles in complex organizations.

Modern economies function and thrive through the market activities of complex organizations, particularly business corporations. With the onset of the industrial revolution in the 18th century, and with the development of technological innovation that continues apace, organizations have evolved into highly efficient mechanisms that dominate present-day market activities. Employees of Dupont, AT&T, and similar corporations scarcely know who their chief executive officer is. Even in the case of charismatic business leaders, such as William Gates of Microsoft and John Welch of General Electric, the figure is remote, while the mythology is too vague for them to become identifiable. They are both so wealthy and powerful as to make them distant figures in the minds of most employees of these corporations.

If we intend to debate and possibly refine Freud's group psychology, we need to examine the influence of the leader on the led in modern corporations, where, at first glance, neither libido nor identification would seem to account for group formations and behavior. Instead, our first impression suggests we look at the role of self-interest in explaining how people perform in designated roles in complex organizations.

I

People enter economic organizations initially as a result of a contract to give services in exchange for pay and benefits. In the case of a senior executive, especially the chief executive officer, the contract is a written document signed by the CEO and the Chairman of the Board. In the case of lower level employees and staff, the contract is verbal but nevertheless the basis for employment. The exchange of services for monetary reward is the platform on which the relationship between the corporation and the individual stands. Noncompliance with the terms of the contract results in the severing of the relationship.

Rewards proliferate if the relationship proves productive. For the corporation, the gains from the abilities and even creativity of an employee may go well beyond the requirements of the job. Individuals give expression to talents and ego interests from which they derive considerable intrinsic satisfactions as well as increased monetary rewards. They may enjoy the associations they develop with colleagues. Indeed, they may participate in elaborate social interactions that cannot be envisioned in the contract and that becomes part of the social fabric defining the corporate body. Sometimes these ancillary memberships may cause harm to the corporation, for example, membership in a labor union that enters into conflict with the corporation on the terms of the contract, leading at times to work stoppages and protracted negotiations harmful to the image of the corporation.

Underlying all the aspects of contractual relationships is self-interest. If an employee can find a job that pays more, offers more interesting work assignments, and perhaps represents more prestigious employment, that employee will probably leave the organization. Mobility may be easier for higher level employees than for lower level employees, yet the same principle underlies expectations: if one can improve one's lot in life, then the rational action is to grasp opportunities as they present themselves. It therefore behooves the organization to encourage capable people to stay. Often those who stay have few, if any, alternatives; consequently, they experience increased dependency and vulnerability to such unfortunate events as plant closings, corporate consolidations, and loss of employment.

Translating the language of contract and economics into a more direct psychological framework, we must recognize that the play in the dynamics of contract and self-interest is in the accumulation and exercise of power. The psychological frame of reference becomes ego psychology, not libido theory. The autonomy of the ego is a direct function of the ability of the individual to garner power and to learn to use it effectively.

When Freud (1921) stated that individuals share a multiplicity of group minds but, "he [the individual] can raise himself above them to the extent of having a scrap of independence and originality" (p. 129), he may have had in mind that the cultivation of talents gains expression through the exercise of power, which often is antithetical to the dependencies that are fostered in group membership.

This "scrap of independence and originality" brings us face-to-face with the nature of power. Power is the potential an individual has to direct and even alter the thinking and behavior of others. Defined this way, power should be distinguished from authority and influence. Authority grants presumptive rights while the individual occupies a position in the organization or is a member of a profession with visible credentials. For authority to become power, the individual must perform significant psychological work in the form of internalizing the sources of authority and accepting their legitimacy without guilt, anxiety, or shame. An individual enacting from this power base is influencing others. Successful enactments result in an accretion to this internalized sense of power. At the same time, the objects of this influence will feel rewarded in both a material and an intrinsic way. Thus, the narcissism of leaders Freud made central to his group psychology has a rational basis beyond the regressive phenomena often attributed to attachment to a narcissistic leader.

Instances abound, however, where the internalized power base becomes irrational when the leader is narcissistic in the pathological sense as a result of either incipient megalomania or a stubborn repetition compulsion. *The New York Times* and *The Wall Street Journal* each carried lead stories on Monday, June 15, 1998 on the firing of the Chief Executive Officer of the Sunbeam Corporation. Albert J. Dunlap had developed a reputation, not in small part as a result of self-promotion, as an expert in increasing the economic value of a corporation to its shareholders. He appeared ruthless and seemed to prize the reputation for "cut, slash, and burn" in reducing costs and restoring profitability to corporations that were languishing. He was known as "Chain Saw Al," having applied his methodology to such corporations as Crown Zellarbach, a lumber concern, and Scott Paper Company. He made a great deal of money for the shareholders and himself in his craft of "turn around," by reducing costs and his willingness to sell assets and even sell entire corporations, as he did when he sold Scott to Kimberly Clark, another paper company.

Dunlap fits Freud's description of the leader who loves no one but himself. His narcissism permits him to cut jobs and dismiss people, since it is sustained by an ego ideal as a ruthless leader working in the economic interests of shareholders, and ultimately himself. Dunlap (1996) has stated publicly and in his book, *Mean Business,* that he is paid to produce results measurable in dollars and cents. The opposite of this ego ideal is the type of chief executive officer who is considerate of his employees and will cause layoffs only with the greatest reluctance. For Dunlap, this compassionate image evokes scorn and contempt.

When Dunlap took the chief executive's job in Sunbeam, a maker of appliances, there were high expectations as the investor community drove up the price of the stock from $12 to $53 per share solely on the basis of the promises implicit in Dunlap's appearance as chief executive officer. Dunlap tripped in his performance at Sunbeam, and there were questionable accounting decisions that appeared to inflate sales and earnings. At this writing, Sunbeam's stock is trading around $8 a share. Many people lost money, including two prominent investors who hold significant amounts of Sunbeam's stock.

Implicitly recognizing the importance of continuity in leadership, boards of directors are reluctant to fire chief executive officers. Traditionally, boards have great difficulty in mobilizing the power to act decisively. They often provide excellent examples of groups at sea without leadership. But, times have changed and boards now focus on accountability, particularly where there are significant shares of stock in the hands of a few investing institutions and entrepreneurs, as is the case in Sunbeam. Underlying the decision to fire Dunlap was the recognition that when a leader fails to perform, demoralization occurs, substantiating Freud's (1921) assertion, "The loss of the leader in some sense or other, *the birth of misgivings about him* brings on the outbreak of panic. . . . the mutual ties between the members of the group disappear, as a rule, at the same time as the tie with their leader" (p. 97).

Perhaps panic is too strong a term to describe the reactions to a leader who is failing and who ultimately is discharged. The better term is anxiety. In formal organizations, in which relationships initially derive from contract and from role definitions that align individuals in some juxtaposition to their leader and the authority structure, the tie to the leader is driven by contractual obligation and its underlying mechanism, self-interest. The ties that develop among peers reporting to the same authority figure are also governed by self-interest, which seems in contradiction to Freud's notion that peers identify with one another as they hold in common their leader in their respective ego ideal. And in this identification it appears that self-interest gives way to common purpose and the well-being of group members. But this contradiction is superficial. The common purpose depends on each individual's fulfilling his obligations in the broad division of labor that characterizes complex organizations. So it is more accurate to say that, to his subordinates, the leader is emblematic of their common purpose and the necessity for the division of labor to function in order to fulfill self-interests. Failure in the division of labor is second only to failure of the authority figure's performance in causing deep anger, anxiety, and despair in the group. Freud's assertion of the primacy of the leader is essentially correct. However, it needs amplification in understanding behavior in complex organizations.

II

"[I]t is impossible to grasp the nature of a group if the leader is disregarded" (Freud, 1921, p. 65).

Leaders in complex organizations are designated. They are placed in positions of formal authority either by appointment or through election according to established rules. Under the terms, stated and unstated, of contractual relationships, subordinates defer to the authority figure as a matter of course. But that this deference to authority becomes power for the leader should not be assumed.

Perhaps the clearest cases of the gap between authority and power are to be found in political organizations. The authority of an office is invested with power only when subordinates attribute their chief's initiatives as supportive of their interests and beliefs. Once these attributes take hold, subordinates will perceive personal power in their superiors and act as though their interests and the chief's are identical. Indeed, the mechanism of identification that Freud referred to as the basis of group cohesion is a direct consequence of an executive's action and the attributions of common interests. Richard Neustadt, Professor of Government at Harvard

University, observed firsthand the office of the President of the United States.

In form, all Presidents are leaders nowadays. In fact, this guarantees no more than they will be clerks. Everybody now expects the man in the White House to do something about everything. Laws and customs now reflect acceptance of him as the Great Initiator, an acceptance quite as wide-spread at the Capital as at his end of Pennsylvania Avenue. But such acceptance does not signify that all the rest of government is at his feet. *It merely signifies that other men have found it practically impossible to do their jobs without assurance of initiatives from him.* Service for themselves, not power for the president, has brought them to accept his leadership in form [Neustadt, 1964, p. 6; italics added].

Unlike political organizations, where office holders frequently establish constituencies and a power base independent of the chief executive, there is more direct and unified authority flowing from the top in corporations. One of the interesting variables in corporate leadership is how the chief executive maintains control of the authority structure. The leader will fail if she inadvertently relinquishes control and permits independent power bases to flourish. Rivalries will ensue and purposes will become diffuse, vitiating whatever initiatives the chief executive seeks to pursue. At the same time, if subordinates feel constrained and have a sense of obsessive control on the part of the chief executive, they will become passive, if not outrightly rebellious and seek employment elsewhere.

An interesting illustration of the quandary facing chief executives in balancing their need for control with the autonomy of subordinates can be seen in the case of a college president. The late social psychologist Douglas McGregor spent most of his career at the Massachusetts Institute of Technology, where he taught theories of group behavior and leadership. But at one point, determined to apply his theories to the practice of leadership, he accepted appointment as President of Antioch College, a position he held for six years. As he was about to leave this post, McGregor (1966) wrote:

Before coming to Antioch, I had observed and worked with top executives as an advisor in a number of organizations. I thought I knew how they felt about their responsibilities and what led them to behave as they did. I even thought I could create a role for myself that would enable me to avoid some of the difficulties they encountered. I was wrong! . . . I believed, for example, that a leader could operate successfully as a kind of advisor to his organization.

I thought I could avoid being a "boss." Unconsciously, I suspect, I hoped to avoid the unpleasant necessity of making difficult decisions, of taking responsibility for one course of action among many uncertain alternatives, of making mistakes and taking the consequences. I thought that maybe I could operate so that everyone would like me—that "good human relations" would eliminate all discord and disappointment. I could not have been more wrong [p. 67].

The conscious awareness of the responsibilities of office, along with the understanding that unused power undermines the authority structure, overcomes the tendency to give way to one's own passive wishes. But it is not simply the desire to use power that supports the authority structure and, in the end, enables subordinates to do their job. The initiatives a chief executive presents must make sense, even create a sense of excitement, if they are to gain the enthusiastic support of subordinates. Passivity in the chief executive can take many forms. One form is leading with process rather than substance.

A newly appointed chief executive in a large corporation called one of his board members for advice. He had decided to engage a major consulting firm to carry out a study of corporate strategy and to advise on new directions for the corporation. The corporation had been substantially weakened with the success of a major competitor and badly needed new initiatives.

The board member suggested to the chief executive that his proposal was unwise. He said to the chief executive, "You are new to the job. In my opinion, you should visit your factories, spend a great deal of time working directly with your subordinates so that you learn firsthand about the business and your key people. Let them get to know you, how you think, and what are your questions and views about the direction of the business. If you bring in outside consultants, they will stand between you and your people. You will be turning over your authority to them, and you will not be able to understand their views or be able to judge directly the quality of the consultants' analyses and recommendations."

The chief executive disregarded the board member's advice and hired the consulting firm. The consultants introduced a process, holding individual and group interviews, ostensibly to draw out key people on their views concerning corporate objectives and strategies. In the course of this process, one person's opinions could not be separated from another's. The organization did not get to know their boss, nor did their views become differentiated and weighed according to their merits. Process overcame substance and, predictably, the consultants offered an incremental set of recommendations that in their totality failed to take account of the real and disturbing problems this corporation faced. The corporation needed radical steps that could have surfaced and been implemented only if the chief executive had assumed control over a proposal for action. This corporation in short order failed and entered bankruptcy, resulting in dislocations and human suffering.

Process is the attempt to engage people in using a methodology ostensibly to identify problems and offer solutions. Examples of process orientations are in the techniques of cost–benefit analysis and the formation of task groups to figure out how to solve problems. Substance is the direct confrontation of problems, under the direction of a leader who takes responsibility at the outset for grounding the problem in the realities of markets, products, and technologies.

People understand substance. Enmeshed in process, they become confused, feel that time in meetings is wasted time, and lose confidence in the authority of the leader.

The most rational reason for attaching oneself to authority is to accomplish work that will provide a tangible reward. What makes authority real and easily converted to power that is accepted and adhered to is the visibility of substantive leadership. Why authority ultimately fails can be found in the understanding of the variable in leadership called character. Freud's *Group Psychology* opens the door to considering the character, including the substantive abilities, of the leader as a variable in understanding behavior in complex organizations.

III

It is a commonplace to observe the variability of the behavior of authority figures. While one may attribute this variability to the differences in situations—assuming that one can readily adapt behavior to meet the requirements of the situation—the weight of the evidence indicates the opposite: how an authority figure behaves is strongly determined by character, the habitual modes of response to internal and external stimuli.

The political scientist Harold Lasswell (1930) published a volume titled *Psychopathology and Politics*. His thesis stated that an authority figure's private conflicts (meaning neurotically determined conflicts) spill over into behavior, decisions, and policies. Lasswell called this phenomenon "private conflicts with public consequences." Thus, students of political behavior ask whether Richard Nixon as President of the United States flooded his perceptions, especially during the Vietnam conflict and later during Watergate, with an underlying paranoid character structure noted by suspicion, mistrust, and the need to objectify the existence of enemies (Wills, 1970).[1] Aside from pathological outcomes of disturbance in character formation, authority figures regularly display character in the constancy of their behavior, their predilection to define problems and the world about them according to certain inner imperatives as well as the objective requirements of the situation. Table 1 connects the individual's dominant orientation (persons, tactics, ideas) with character (passive, reactive, and active).

The terms Homeostatic, Mediative, and Proactive in the diagonal of Table 1 suggest modes of behavior, commonly referred to as styles of leadership. The first, homeostatic, indicates that the authority figure takes as his goal maintaining the steady state of the organization, to restore equilibrium following a disturbance either from within or outside of the organization. Mediative refers to the direction of activity toward moderating the effects of a disturbance from outside the organization, causing adaptation within to meet the external conditions. Proactive is the use of the organization's resources to change the environment. Here, the vision comes first and the use of the organization's resources second, implying the uses of a leader's abilities and imagination to redefine situations and the goals of the organization. In other terms, the first two categories refer to what managers do, the third to what leaders do (Zaleznik, 1992).

In the absence of flagrant pathologies of character, it is difficult to discern the workings of Lasswell's (1930) formula, where private conflicts

---

1. Rangell (1980) takes as his object of study not only the leader, in this case Nixon, but also the group in the relation between the leader and the led.

Table 1. Orientation and character in leadership style.

Dominant Orientation	Character		
	Passive	Reactive	Active
Persons	Homeostatic		
Tactics		Mediative	
Ideas			Proactive

determine actions, with serious public consequences. One can speculate, but seldom can one observe the clear-cut display of neuroses determining a leader's behavior. There are such diverse reality issues as to obscure what is purely conflict-driven behavior. Furthermore, the structure of roles in organizations and the diffusion of power bases within these roles protect the organization against megalomania and other abuses of power.

In the case of complex organizations, particularly large enterprises, one has to magnify observation to discern the pathologies of group psychology and the behavior of the leader. The lead to follow is Acton's (1948) axiom: Power tends to corrupt; absolute power corrupts absolutely (p. 25). But what is the corrupting influence of power?

Pathologies are most readily displayed in family-owned and family-managed organizations. In those organizations, the protective barriers to neurotic displays scarcely exist, and therefore we have almost a test-tube sample of psychological regression and group pathologies in relation to, or in the absence of, a leader.

IV

"Thus, social feeling is based upon the reversal of what was first a hostile feeling into a positively-toned tie in the nature of an identification" (Freud, 1921, p. 121).

Implicit throughout *Group Psychology* is Freud's recognition of the tenuous nature of the ties among group members. In the case of siblings, love and compassion arise from negative feelings. Only when parents have been incorporated in the ego ideal is identification with siblings solidified and hostile feelings repressed. But the latent hostility does not disappear. It is subject to renewed intensity when events undermine the fragile myth that all siblings or peers are equal. Freud's formula for social justice, "that we deny ourselves many things so that others may have to do without them as well" (p. 121), conflicts with reality, particularly where siblings or peers act out the myth of equality in corporate affairs. This myth prevents leadership from emerging and acting in the world of economic competition. The ultimate failure of family enterprises can be directly attributed to the inability of siblings to grant authority to one of their members and to allow this individual to function as a leader. Leadership cannot work without the spontaneous willingness of others to accept differentials in power and accede to an authority figure. Much is made in the sociological literature of the concept of legitimacy of authority.[2] The psychodynamic underpinning of legitimacy is the internalization of power differentials in harmony with ego interests and in recognition that, in its absence, individuals cannot function in consonance with their abilities.

For example, a retail enterprise of some magnitude thrived as a group of four brothers worked together over many years to build the business. The brothers seemed to differentiate themselves according to talents and interests and managed to cooperate under the leadership of the eldest. Although he behaved harshly and often impetuously, the younger siblings complied and seemed to tolerate his eccentricities. As time passed, the siblings brought into the business their sons and sons-in-law, who with few exceptions were not distinguished in their abilities, nor especially entrepreneurial. As the original siblings aged, the question of transferring authority loomed larger in their thinking and became a cause for concern. They decided to seek consultation.

The consultant discovered a deep difference of perception between the two generations. The older generation, the siblings who founded the business, were in despair over the fact that the so-called juniors, men well into their 40s and 50s, showed little initiative. The juniors believed they were hamstrung by the seniors, that they were not permitted to innovate or show initiative despite the fact that the youngest of this second generation had decided to start a new type of retail chain and received support from the seniors. He managed to build this venture into a significant and profitable business. It was as though what this youngest of the peer group had done could not enter consciousness and be dealt with in the face of the juniors' belief that they were being held back by the seniors. The

---

2. See Talcott Parsons, *Structure and Process in Modern Societies*. Glencoe, IL: The Free Press, 1960, pp. 20–21.

function of this belief was to maintain the illusion of equality in every sense of the word, including parity in compensation.

The consultant broke into this myth with a written report recommending a new organization structure that accorded authority to two peers drawn from the younger generation, one as chairman and chief executive, and the other as president and chief operating officer. The consultant presented his logic for this differentiation by pointing out the debilitating effects of maintaining the myth of equality in decision making and preventing nonfamily executives from doing their jobs energetically.

At a group meeting of the two generations and the consultant to consider the report and its recommendations, the wife of one of the younger peers, obviously incensed that her husband was to become subordinate to the chairman and president, appeared and asked to attend the meeting. When asked, the consultant said it would not be appropriate for her to attend, so she left the meeting much to her chagrin and her husband's embarrassment.

The consultant, summarizing his report and recommendations, pointed to the harmful effects on the business of the unrealistic commitment to equality. The peers, accusing him of being dictatorial, launched into an attack on the consultant. One of the peers called him an "ayatollah," who was much in the news with the overthrow of the Shah of Iran.

During the angry rejection of the consultant and his report, the seniors remained silent. The juniors asked the consultant to leave while they deliberated on what they should do. The consultant later received a call from one of the juniors, who reported that the group had agreed to burn all copies of the report and to continue as though the report did not exist and had never been presented. About a year later, the consultant received a call to report that the group had decided to adopt his recommendations, to appoint from their number a chairman and a president, and to make other changes enlarging the scope of a few nonfamily executives.

Several years later, the company declared itself bankrupt and entered liquidation. From reports he received, the consultant learned that the business could not overcome competition that had vigorous leadership and a highly adaptive organization. This sorry outcome was an example of "too little, too late."

What one often observes in such family enterprises is collective denial implicit in group process and the tacit agreement to avoid conflict, in support of a mythology. In Freud's (1911) study of the Schreber case, he commented that observers often mistake the effort at cure for the illness itself, indicating that the delusion symptoms are a defense against a more catastrophic regression. In the same vein, the group formations that arise in support of a mythology defend against serious regression and the outbreak of overt aggression characteristic of sibling rivalry. The resulting equilibrium, however, includes a more fundamental denial of the need for leadership. This need has to be measured against the challenges of market economics where the end game is survival.

V

"If therefore in groups narcissistic self-love is subject to limitations which do not operate outside them, that is cogent evidence that the essence of a group formation consists in new kinds of libidinal ties among the members of the group" (Freud, 1921, p. 103).

Narcissism, or self-love, seemingly stands in opposition to object love. In the cases of hypnosis or falling in love, the object is overvalued and the ego undergoes some depletion. In complex organizations, the contradiction between narcissism and object love often disappears. The ego becomes enhanced through the phenomenon of membership. The enhancement occurs not simply as a result of the feeling of belonging, as occurs, for example, in elite military groups or prestigious professional societies. Because complex organizations provide a multiplicity of rewards, the appearance of a surplus in gratifications reverberates back into the overvaluation of the organization and the increase in self-esteem as a result of being a member.

As is the case in so many aspects of human experience, gratifications that appear to be permanent often prove to be illusory. Therefore, it pays to heed Freud's implicit warning about group membership: "each individual therefore has a share in numerous group minds [upon which he builds up his ego ideal]. . . . he can also raise himself above them to the extent of having a scrap of independence and originality" (p. 78).

There is an exchange constantly in play as a condition of group membership. In exchange for dedication to the group's purpose and division of labor, acceptance of authority and its directives, and a generalized willingness to put the interests of the group above self-interest, the member enjoys an accretion to his narcissism. This aspect of self-esteem can be viewed as institutional narcissism, the derivative of belonging.

As recent times have shown, narcissistic advantage that comes from belonging may in the long-term harm the institution as well as the individual. Like individuals, institutions have a history and produce a legacy that enters into the exchange of devotion to the group for accretions to self-esteem. Yet whether the institution will endure has far less to do with the loyalty it demands and achieves from its members than the capacity of the organization to abide by the logic of the reality principle.

Competitive advantage is not self-perpetuating in economic organizations. The advantages of one period in its history do not assure continuing success—times change, consumer preferences shift, and products that appeal today may fall out of favor tomorrow.

For Henry Ford, his work was complete in 1916 with the development of the Model T and the assembly line. He bitterly resisted efforts, even on the part of his son Edsel, to change the product to meet new preferences in style and function that the head of General Motors, Alfred Sloan, had conceptualized and solidified in his formulation of product segmentation. Mr. Sloan was quick to identify the weaknesses in Ford's product philosophy ("We will give the consumer any color he desires so long as the car is black") and to develop an organization structure (decentralization of operations and centralization of financial controls) best suited to the broadening of product lines to support market segmentation. General Motors overtook Ford and became the successful model of the modern corporation while the Ford Motor Company barely escaped bankruptcy.

A deep and unrecognized psychological shift occurred in General Motors. The power elite of the corporation internalized Sloan's policies so that they became the fixed guidelines for the ongoing function of the organization. Leadership succession came from within the corporation. It would only be a slight overstatement of the case to suggest that Sloan and his philosophy became the symbol of success while the organization became a totemistic community. The dynamic that perpetuated this community was the fulfillment of the promise of institutional narcissism. To belong to General Motors as a high-level executive meant wealth, prestige, and the enjoyment of self-esteem. It was not so far-fetched to take as the ultimate expression of institutional narcissism what Charles E. Wilson, then chief executive officer of General Motors, declared before a Congressional committee, "What's good for General Motors is good for America."

Forces are constantly at work to undermine the gains of institutional narcissism. In the case of General Motors, for example, the rise of the Japanese automobile industry accounted for a loss of market share from 50% to 30% during the period 1950 to 1998. GM simply lost track of consumer desires while it remained fixated on large, gas-guzzling cars. The Japanese car makers filled a product niche at the expense mainly of General Motors.

Another weakening effect of institutional narcissism is that it generally favors the power elite, usually excluding staff outside the ranks of the elite. In a study of stress reactions in the Canadian Broadcasting Corporation, undertaken at the request of top management concerned about the high incidence of reported stress illnesses, it was found that members of the power elite were less prone to stress symptoms than were other operating and staff people. The researchers explained this result by pointing to the protective, cocoonlike effects of belonging to the elite as a barrier to stress (Zaleznik, Kets de Vries, and Howard, 1977).

Some outside agency, such as bankers or the investment community, is usually required to break into the self-satisfaction that permeates institutional narcissism at the expense of long-term corporate development. Outside agencies press for change in leadership, usually by bringing in a chief executive officer from outside the corporation. These new leaders often have a sense of what needs to be done, including engaging people in a symbolic form of patricide—destroying the totem representative of leadership from the past. This symbolic enactment of the oedipal drama breaks the ties to the past and frees individuals to think objectively rather than in the customary modes that are bound into the experience of institutional narcissism.

VI

"[A] neurosis should make its victim asocial, and should remove him from the usual group formations. It may be said that a neurosis has the same disintegrating effect upon a group as being in love. On the other hand it appears that where a powerful impetus has been given to group formation neuroses may diminish and, at all events temporarily, disappear" (Freud, 1921, p. 142).

The neurosis that stands at the end of a chain that extends from being in love, to hypnosis, to group formation is the Oedipus complex and the myth of the primal horde, in which the youngest son takes credit for killing the tyrannical father and succeeds him as leader. Group parricide is repressed in the formation of a totemistic community in which the slain father is introjected and symbolized in the group's totem. The youngest son frees himself from the constraints of the group as a condition for assuming leadership. Thus, Freud asserts, individual psychology emerged from group psychology with the myth of the hero, whom Freud calls an epic poet.

Like all other aspects of the unconscious, sexual longings and the aggressive component of the Oedipus complex may be repressed and, as Freud further argued, safely repressed under the conditions of group membership. But the impulses, both sexual and aggressive, and the longings for the power of the leader are not dissolved and forever gone. Not only does the Oedipus complex reappear at various stages of development, such as adolescence, but also it must be resolved anew if maturation is to occur. Psychoanalytic theory holds to a tragic view of the individual. No problem is settled once and for all; no victory is achieved, never ancient conflicts permanently resolved. Opposed to this tragic view is the Utopian view that takes progress as its measure of man's inherent goodness and capacity for growth. Historically, the principles underlying this faith in progress have been technological or humanistic, offering ideological solutions to the problem of power and authority so vividly described in Freud's references to the Oedipus complex and the hero myth. This optimism has reached into the mode of governing human relations in complex organizations.

The central issue in the technological and the humanistic solutions alike is the orientation to authority. In the technological solution, subordination to authority becomes depersonalized. While there is an organizational hierarchy, the logic of efficiency places all individuals in the position of subordinating their personal goals to a superordinate methodology variously called scientific management, managerial controls, or professional management. Thus, sophisticated budgeting procedures formalize goals to which people become committed and are held accountable. Accountability is not to another individual in the hierarchy, but to goals arrived at objectively but never at the risk of having one person impose his will on another. If power is the potential that one individual has to cause another to alter his thinking and behavior in a direction that the other would not have otherwise taken, then, under modern managerial technology, the relations become devoid of power or, if not devoid, consciously muted.

Scientific management, which grew out of the tortured genius of Frederick Winslow Taylor at the turn of the 20th century, presupposes that goals can be minutely defined, communicated, and achieved by applying consistent techniques in the work place. A worker at a lathe machining metal is not told person-to-person how to work. The directives are depersonalized and the behavior constrained by the methodology of work that is explicit and carefully drawn from an expertise that itself is distant and impersonal. Against whom is the individual to vie? Scientific management substituted programmed efficiency for personal directives under which one person with greater power than his subordinates could determine the behavior of those subordinates at the risk of sanctions. In a sense, the group psychology underpinning compliance with the methodology of efficiency depends on members of a work group identifying with one another and forming cohesive groups. The cohesion grows out of the sense of equal deprivation in that all members of the group are subject to the same principles governing their behavior. If it is autonomy they want, they had best seek a contract other than the one governing their employment. On the other hand, they do not feel oppressed by tyrannical leadership, nor do they suffer the humiliation of being told what to do in a personal relationship with an authority figure. This methodology governing authority relationships applies to all levels of the power structure except that at higher levels the identification is with a profession called management. Feeling a part of this profession and enacting the principles on which managerial behavior is sustained supports an ego ideal and the mutual identifications of like-minded members who have internalized this ego ideal.

Wandering through the halls of large corporations and into the meeting rooms where group members interact, one can listen to the language of professional management and discover the low level of emotion governing behavior. Anyone becoming angry and showing it is liable to be perceived as a person prone to losing control. Displays of aggression, particularly directed toward another person, will suffer opprobrium as "abrasive." If decisions go against one's wishes and disappointment becomes evident, one will gain the reputation of "taking things personally."

These rules governing behavior in a cohesive professional group result from enactment of a role and the suppression of emotion, along with the repression of conflicts with authority such as would appear in oedipal anxiety. Complex organizations are not hospitable to the neuroses.

Humanistic approaches to complex organizations view with alarm the depersonalization of power that goes hand and glove with the technologist's programmatic control of behavior. For many students of complex organizations with a bent for normative changes, the target is power and hierarchy. Deaf to the notion that hierarchy is a form found in nature, with applicability to human beings as well as to animals, humanistic psychologists propose, if not the total elimination of hierarchy, the flattening of the power pyramid. They also propose the transfer of power from upper to lower levels of the organization. The theme is empowerment of subordinates. The psychological premises of empowerment are twofold: first, the individual's sense of autonomy is heightened, along with the feeling that his choices have multiplied; second, now that he is a member of a group with increased power, his membership enhances his sense of autonomy and pride in the group.

The main problem with this humanistic effort at eliminating power struggles and the ambivalence arising from inequality in the distribution of power is the lack of evidence to support the premises. Experiments in the alteration of power relationships, either through redistribution or creating more benign authority figures in primary groups go back as far as 1927.[3] None of the findings of major experiments persist to this day. The empirical evidence suggests that the experiments sooner or later fell victim to the reality that productivity does not sustain initial increases that result from, usually, a kind of euphoria reminiscent of how a person feels under the sway of a strong positive transference. In a broader sense, the experiments fail because of such reality factors as major changes in markets, product preferences, and cost structures. During the summer of 1998, the strike at General Motors, which resulted in massive plant shut downs, involved deep issues arising from loss of jobs to foreign markets, such as Mexico, where labor costs are substantially less than in Flint,

---

3. See Elton Mayo, *The Human Problems of an Industrialization,* 2nd edition. Boston: Division of Research, Graduate School of Business, 1946 (originally published in 1933).

Michigan, and other United States locations. Authority tends to respond to market forces, which, in turn, tend to drive out considerations concerning the humanization of power.

There are other, more subtle issues to consider in the lingering questions of authority and power in complex organizations. What are the consequences of rising expectations concerning the distribution of authority? Social experiments in complex organizations must recognize the possibilities of unanticipated consequences of action. When social experiments humanistically driven fall under the weight of the reality principle, one should expect a diminished sense that authority is rational. Not only do identifications weaken, but anxiety heightens because the behavior of authority falls under the cloud of questionable motives and distorted logic.

If students of complex organizations turn to Freud's *Group Psychology* to find answers about the governing of men and women, they will be sorely disappointed. The questions are plentiful, but, in keeping with the traditions of psychoanalysis, the answers are few and complex.

In his book *Progress and Revolution,* psychoanalyst Robert Waelder (1967) disclaims being either conservative or liberal in his convictions. In giving a rough sketch of his views on broad issues of power and human aspirations, Waelder cites an example taken from education:

> There is a story of an Edwardian lady who said to the governess: 'Miss X, go into the garden, see what the children are doing, and stop them from doing it.' This in essence is the conservative approach. The liberal approach would be somewhat like this: 'See what the children are doing and help them do it.' . . . [But] both approaches will, in the majority of cases, lead to unwelcome consequences [pp. ix, x].

One need not be in a state of despair as a conservative nor starry-eyed as a liberal concerning man's uneasy relationship to power. If one accepts, however tentatively, Freud's primacy of the leader in group psychology, attention then turns to how organizations and society assure the presence and quality of leadership. Leaders are not born; rather, they emerge as a result of personal development, education, and training. Such institutions as universities, professional schools, military academies, corporations, and governments select pools of able people without any guarantees that they are selecting people who will become leaders. Leaders will emerge given the force of personal ambition. What these institutions finally do in the preparation of able people and would-be leaders is to expand ego interests, hone competencies, and deepen the quality of mind.

REFERENCES

Acton, J. (1948), *Essays on Freedom and Power*. Boston: Beacon Press, pp. 25, 28.

Dunlap, A. J. (1996), *Mean Business: How I Save Bad Companies and Make Good Companies Great*. New York: Times Business.

Freud, S. (1911), Psycho-analytic notes on an autobiographical account of a case of paranoia (dementia paranoides). *Standard Edition,* 12: 3–82. London: Hogarth Press, 1958.

Freud, S. (1921), *Group Psychology and the Analysis of the Ego. Standard Edition,* 18:69–143. London: Hogarth Press, 1955.

Lasswell, H. (1930), *Psychopathology and Politics*. Chicago: University of Chicago Press.

Lewin, K., Lippit, L. & White, R. (1939), Patterns of aggressive behavior in experimentally created social climates. *J. Soc. Psychol.,* 10:271–299.

McGregor, D. (1966), *Leadership and Motivation*. Cambridge, MA: MIT Press.

Mead, G. H. (1956), Self, mind, and society. In: *The Social Psychology of George Herbert Mead,* ed. A. Strauss. Chicago: University of Chicago Press, pp. 128–294.

Neustadt, R. E. (1964), *Presidential Power: The Politics of Leadership*. New York: Wiley.

Rangell, L. (1980), *The Mind of Watergate: An Exploration of the Compromise of Integrity*. New York: Norton.

Waelder, R. (1967), *Progress and Revolution: A Study of the Issues of Our Age*. New York: International Universities Press.

Whyte, W. F. (1943), *Street Corner Society*. Chicago: University of Chicago Press.

Wills, G. (1970). *Nixon Agonistes: The Crisis of the Self-Made Man*. Boston: Houghton Mifflin. See also Rangell, L. (1980).

Zaleznik, A. (1956), *Worker Satisfaction and Development: A Case Study of Work and Social Behavior in a Factory Group*. Cambridge, MA: Harvard University, Division of Research, Graduate School of Business Administration.

Zaleznik, A. (1992), Managers and leaders: Are they different? *Harvard Business Rev.,* March–April, pp. 126–135.

Zaleznik, A., Kets de Vries, M. & Howard, J. (1977), Stress reactions in organizations: Syndromes, causes, and consequences. *Behav. Sci.,* May.

Groups and Fanaticism

ANDRÉ E. HAYNAL

In the memory of my father
who earned the Yad Vashem distinction

and of my Uncle Teddy Mahler
who hardly escaped
the destiny prepared for him
by the fanatics

As we know, Freud opened many doors. The resulting insights were embodied, for example, in the works in which he helped us to understand life "in groups"—that is, in society (Freud, 1927, 1930). Freud (1921) himself says that only "under certain exceptional conditions is individual psychology in a position to disregard the relations of this individual to others" (p. 69). He also points out that the question of individual psychology arises after this natural connection[1] has been severed. This theme certainly pervades his other writings as well, since sexuality is conceived together with its "object," and man, too, is ultimately always placed in a context with the Other.

Freud's contribution on group psychology in 1921 falls midway between the *Three Essays* (1905) and *Instincts and Their Vicissitudes* (1915c), on the one hand, and the major works on culture and civilization—*The Future of an Illusion* (1927) and *Civilization and Its Discontents* (1930)—on the other. In retrospect, it is surely appropriate after a century of manmade disasters to pay more heed to his message. Among the phenomena that loomed large in the sorry history of the 20th century, fanaticism

---

Translated from French by Philip Slotkin.

1. Strachey's rendering of Freud's word *Zusammenhang* by "continuity" is inaccurate.

occupies an important position. What contribution can psychoanalysis make, in particular along the pathway opened up by Freud (1921) with his *Group Psychology and the Analysis of the Ego,* to elucidating these phenomena?

Let us begin by recalling the importance of the ego ideal, to which Freud here draws attention and which accounts for a wide range of manifestations, such as the fascination of love, dependence on a hypnotist, and submission to a leader. *Group Psychology* is ultimately a *political* work that came into being in the aftermath of the World War I and, in particular, of the breakup of the Austro-Hungarian Empire, events that deprived Freud and many of his coworkers—who, like him, came from its peripheral regions—of their ancestral roots. "Little Austria" was born, and Freud exclaimed in a letter to Ferenczi dated March 17, 1919: "It is painful to think that more or less the whole world will be a foreign country" (Freud, 1996). During the reign of Franz Joseph I in the closing years of the 19th century, Vienna witnessed not only an exceptional explosion of culture, science, and art, but also the fulfillment—however imperfect—of the ideals of pluralism, tolerance, and multilingualism. This Vienna was Freud's country, of which he was fond, although his attachment to it was admittedly ambivalent. *Group Psychology and the Analysis of the Ego* may have been only a stage in his mourning. The work of mourning gives rise to an effort to understand. Freud himself wrote in a letter to Romain Rolland on March 4, 1923: "Not that I regard this work as particularly successful, but it does demonstrate the path from analysis of the individual to the understanding of society" (Vermorel and Vermorel, 1993, p. 219). It is worth emphasizing the word society, which the rendering of *Massen*—the masses—in English as "groups" fails to convey. Gustave Le Bon's (1895) *La Psychologie des Foules,* on which Freud draws, also referred to *foules* (crowds), a notion close to masses and not to groups. Le Bon examined the relationship between the crowd and the inciter—which is tantamount, in the extreme, to that between the fanaticizer and the fanaticized. The fact that nonmembers of the group, whose status as such represents a danger to its cohesion, are viewed with hostility or even hatred is also noted. Furthermore, the concepts of the instincts, "identification," "ego differentiation," and the "ego ideal" allow us to examine the phenomena of social life and also, in particular, that of fanaticism. Jacques Lacan (1956) pointed out that Freud "closely anticipates fascist organizations," while Jean-Bertrand Pontalis (1968) mentioned "an initial psychological explanation—in advance—of Nazism." Even so, while Freud was composing this text, the Bolshevik regime was establishing itself in the Soviet Union, and religious authoritarianism was casting its shadow in Austria, in particular in the form of the 1930s clerical semifascism of Chancellors Dollfuss and Schuschnigg.

* * *

Arthur Koestler (1978) notes that the 20th century spawned Hitlerism, Stalinism, and Maoism, whereas, for example, the sixth century B.C. saw the flourishing of Taoism, Confucianism, and Buddhism. According to Haldane (1932), fanaticism first appeared in our culture between 3000 B.C. and A.D. 1400.[2] The so-called prophetic religions (Judaism, Christianity, and Islam) are also said to have been more inclined to give rise to fanatical phenomena—because of their claim to possess the one and only Truth—than is, for example, Buddhism, which leaves room for much greater uncertainty as to the fundamental data of human existence. In his examination of the Church that he knew—the Roman Catholic form of Christianity born of the Counterreformation and supported by the House of Habsburg—Freud clearly analyzed the interplay of forces that molded this religious and political phenomena.

Can psychoanalysis contribute to the understanding of the propensity to fanaticism, which has for so long poisoned our culture and civilization? Can psychoanalysis throw light on the foundations within the individual psyche of the forces that impel man, perhaps every one of us, to become fanatical?

The importance of this phenomenon and of its destructive force remained unrecognized for a very long time. Aside from a few sages such as Spinoza, no one had used the concept of fanaticism prior to the Enlightenment. Attempts to understand fanaticism are thus inseparable from the European culture and civilization of the last few centuries.

The 18th-century *philosophes* were the first to employ the concept in a wider sense. Consideration of fanaticism came into its own primarily

---

2. "Between 3000 B.C. and A.D. 1400 there were probably only four really important inventions, namely the general use of iron, paved roads, voting, and religious intolerance . . . which was possibly invented by the Jews, and independently by the Zoroastrian Persians" (Haldane, 1932, pp. 49, 51).

for the condemnation of religious zealotry. Such zealotry is the antithesis of Enlightenment and Reason—and, in the last analysis, of tolerance, pluralism, and freedom of thought. The word fanaticism comes from the Latin *fanum* (temple) and is applied to any excessive or delusional manifestations of allegiance to a religion or form of religion that would nowadays be called fundamentalist. The religion denounced by the *philosophes* and by Voltaire—Christianity in the form of the Roman Catholicism of the Cardinals and other allies of the French monarchy—was the one responsible for the Inquisition within Europe and for the expeditions that substantially wiped out other civilizations elsewhere in the world. With the subsequent progressive decline in faith, hitherto dominant Christian religions were replaced by the great secular religions and all kinds of utopias, which were hailed as the advent of the Kingdom of Heaven—albeit in this case on earth: nationalism/chauvinism; National Socialism/Hitlerism; communism/Stalinism/Maoism/Pol Potism; and the like. Finally, the new religious observances reproduced the forms of fanaticism, especially in the sects that have continued to spread like wildfire even at the end of our own century, following the collapse of the various secular doctrines (such as Nazism and communism).

What is the reason for the resounding *appeal* of fanaticism and for its profound attraction? It reposes on an intellectual system that declares itself, in the name either of a divinity or of other acknowledged authorities, such as Science in our own day, to be in possession of the one and only Truth: "That is how it is because Science has proved it" and "That is how it is because our knowledge comes direct from the Divinity." Such assertions afford narcissistic exaltation and even enormous security: "We are *in possession* of the Truth." That calls for the "sacrifice of the intellect," as in the formula *credo quia absurdum* (I believe because it is absurd). In other words, every possibility of doubt and questioning, or of the emergence of a new point of view—that is to say any analysis of (external or internal) reality—is cast aside. This is part of what fanaticism portrays as a possible *loss* to the individual and to society. In a fanatical society, reality is no longer analyzed; fanaticism persists to the point of collapse, when the flames of war or the economic facts of life destroy the "Empire" based on it (whether it be that of Hitler or Stalin or its nationalist variant, as in Bosnia or Kosovo). The absurd genocide in which millions of Cambodians were massacred by the Khmer Rouge in the name of a mystical tabula rasa (prior to the edification of an intangible utopia); the "inexplicable" collective suicide of 900 followers of the Reverend Jim Jones in the Guyanan jungle; Ayatollah Khomeini's bloody Islamic revolution, which banned music and mixed bathing and ordered the shooting of homosexuals; the excesses of the French Revolution, which threatened to destroy Lyon simply because it was not Jacobin enough—all these examples bear witness to the overwhelming force, danger, and destructiveness of this emotional short-circuiting of problems that deserve to be *analyzed* and solved by *rational* means. Everything becomes simple in the fanatic's regressive state: there is good and there is bad (cf. Melanie Klein); the good are ourselves, the Group of the Elect; and the bad are the others, because they do not believe our words.

A Manichaean division of the world into the good and the wicked—a reduction of the polyphonic to the binary—has often featured in religious discourse: the Christian tradition of the *Civitas Dei*, St. Augustine's Kingdom of Heaven versus the pagan "World," is an example that has persisted in all Christian traditions, whether Catholic or Reformed.

As the foregoing has clearly shown, however, this intellectual structure cannot exist without powerful underlying affective forces. It is in this respect that Freud showed us that the identification with the leader, the quasi-hypnotic submission to his voice, and the projection of all our hopes and ideals onto him are the beginning of a process that enables us to live among "good" people, the Righteous, ourselves, thanks to the immense, so to speak supernatural, wisdom of the leader. Whether this wisdom be, once again, in the name of a divinity, of science, or of the leader's incontrovertible genius, the horde of brothers is safe and secure. There is no more doubt, no more questioning, and no more intellectual or other effort; the solution offered promises paradise, either on earth (as in the different "utopianisms") or in the Beyond (as in the religious variants).

Such distancing from reality may assume truly delusional forms. Again, personal identity in certain situations of generalized societal anxiety is called so greatly into question that the casting of doubt on either it or its justification gives rise to manifestations of self-defensive aggression, as a result of the opening of narcissistic wounds and the threat to self-image and everything invested in it. The outcome is phenomena of extraordinary violence. Entire countries put to fire and sword; untold millions massacred, for example, in religious wars—the ghastliest ever waged by humanity—down the ages; and the havoc wreaked by the secular religions of the 20th century: all these bear eloquent witness to the truth of this statement.

How can fanatical phenomena come into being and crystalize during the course of history? Bolterauer's (1975) distinction between the "primal fanatic" (or "fanaticizer") and the "induced fanatic" is relevant in this context. The fanaticizer, who conceives the fanatical idea or, in a quasi-religious conversion, is among the first to succumb to it, induces others to fall into the same fanatical state of mind. In this way the idea not only becomes legitimate or credible—and, as stated, gives rise to quasi–"self"-defensive aggression (defense of the subject's fragile narcissism invested in the idea, the leader, and the fanatical group)—but also lifts the last inhibitions imposed by the cultural superego of the environment and of the ambient and educational traditions, in a rebellion against an unsatisfactory state of affairs that may perfectly well exist; the quest for a perfect state, following the fanaticizer's emotional appeals, allows the superego to be *repressed* (Rangell, 1974). By virtue of the rationalization that justifies the violation of moral precepts (for example, "We are killing for the good of mankind"), the "righteous" man, from the point of view of the fanaticizing idea, not only indulges in incredible megalomania (Hitler) or suffers from its repercussions in the form of paranoid persecution (Stalin), but also breaches any taboo stemming from the superego or the ego ideal. Oedipal frustrations and the subsequent mourning work they necessitate (Chasseguet-Smirgel, 1975; Chasseguet-Smirgel and Grunberger, 1969) are short-circuited by enactments and perverse solutions, now legitimized by the fanaticizing idea. Wilhelm Reich (1933) long ago described the dynamic of a man who cannot accept his fundamental nature and attempts to get rid of it by assigning it to the Jews, the Gypsies, or the greedy and rapacious bourgeois, thereby expelling what properly belongs to him—namely, a fundamental nature full of sexual and aggressive wishes, which, however, can be cast aside through fanatical ideas.

The historical success of fanaticism is, of course, also linked to the state of society. The messianic voice of a fanaticizer is heard only if it meets with an expectation in the wretched condition of society, whose plight may be economic or have to do with the society's ideals, beliefs, and acceptance—subject, for some authors, to the existence of a potential for "self-fanaticization." The theories of *charisma* (Weber, 1947) and of *prestige* (Le Bon, 1895) were attempts to explain the mysterious power of demagogues—the most perfect example for both authors being Napoleon—to fascinate other people while at the same time paralyzing their judgment. Mohammed's legitimacy, after all, is based wholly on his direct relationship, that is, without an intermediary, with the Ineffable One, God. Weber (1947) described charisma as "a certain quality of an individual personality by virtue of which he is set apart from ordinary men and treated and endowed with supernatural, superhuman, or at least specifically exceptional qualities" (p. 329). Freud interprets these phenomena as projection of the ego ideal of the subject onto the charismatic person. Under the influence of Le Bon (1895), Weber (1947) added that the charismatic authority is fragile and is maintained only by constant demonstration of the leader's strength and successes. Mythological themes, such as betrayal of the leader, sometimes merely add to his fascination. The parallel with hypnosis, as suggested by Freud, is telling. In George Steiner's (1981) novel *The Portage to San Cristobal of A. H.,* the warnings given to the Israeli commandos responsible for conveying a prisoner— who is none other than Hitler—through the equatorial forest are based on these themes: "You must not let him speak. . . . If he is allowed to speak he will trick you and escape. . . . Look away from his eyes. They say that his eyes have a strange light" (p. 33f.).

Aside from these variant forms of the phenomena concerned, the "strange light" incidentally takes us back to the etymology of charisma: the Greek word *kharis* means *that which shines* and physically gladdens the eye: the external grace of a person, a face or a look. Fanaticism comprises an exaltation of the greatness of the cause and its unique, messianic character. Consequently, devotion rests on the faithful as a duty, and the image of perfidy brands traitors and opponents. The similarity of language between different worlds and periods is indeed striking. Everywhere the purity of the believer is contrasted with the impurity of the enemy, health with sickness, God-as-Idea with the scheming designs of Satan. The traitors who are shot or otherwise slain are rabid dogs in the terminology of Teheran just as they are in the records of the Moscow trials or in Rajk's indictment in Budapest, in the same way as everywhere the executioner is the Avenging Angel brandishing Gabriel's sword, kindling the purifying fire or striking a blow with the Fist of the People. Although the images are modified slightly with a few brush strokes through the ages, they always suggest the retributive omnipotence of the Righteous, appropriated from the gods.

Words are accompanied by gestures. The discourse of fanaticism is a communication made up of both language and gestures: the body quakes, jerks upright, and convulses as the orator shouts and roars. A detailed study may one day reveal the weird mimetic activity of fanaticism to have borrowed its gesticulations from mental illness and the ritual dances of "savages" by disinhibition and shamans.

If all this is but caricature, and if Freud causes us to penetrate into these shadow regions of man's subterranean life, including our own civilization, what might be the benefits of such a penetration? They, of course, include a better knowledge of history, a greater ability to resist the temptations of all kinds of totalitarianism, which is the antechamber of fanaticism, and a deeper understanding of those who move in such antechambers or wish to get rid of their fanatical side—that much is certain. But not the least of these benefits is *the ability to recognize the fanatical temptations in ourselves.*

The more a science is surrounded by uncertainties, the less conclusive its proofs, and the greater the predomination of hypotheses over theses, then the more the science—psychoanalysis included—may be corrupted. Our attempt at working through deep human problems on a cultural level by means of a profound interpersonal experience called (by Freud) a psychoanalytic "cure" (*Kur*) and condensing the acquired experience into a theory of conscious or unconscious mental functioning is such an effort. Our temptation or wish to find something more certain and more tangible grows stronger, and, as a result, we may easily find ourselves in a position of defending our "truth" come hell or high water and feel persecuted by all who are not prepared to accept our arguments. We may come to see the world as divided into good, fair-minded, and reasonable people—our brothers and sisters—on one hand, and, on the other, bad people, who demand more evidence, display skepticism, attempt alternative forms of discourse, attack us, and call us into question. Our group is so warm, our ego ideal (Freud's) so reassuring, that anyone who lays hands on this image becomes an enemy, whereas those insiders who suggest changes to the "religion" become, in the language of totalitarian politics, revisionists, worthy only of expulsion—the unconscious wish being to keep the group pure, homogeneous, and worthy of the projected ego ideal, to distinguish ourselves from all the "bad" that is projected outside. While perhaps this may be only a temptation, it is nonetheless one to which we have come close to yielding, explicitly or implicitly, during the course of our history.

* * *

Might the very conception of the "psychoanalytic movement" not be said to contain the seeds of such a tendency? We may well wonder. At the end of the first decade of the 20th century and in the early years of its second decade, notwithstanding the professorship he had finally obtained, Freud found himself excluded from the university. Nor was he sufficiently reassured of the acceptance and the validity of his science. His membership in the B'nai Brith (a Jewish cultural association), the only society he regularly frequented, gave him a kind of sounding board, but nonetheless he remained somewhat ambivalent toward it (Freud to Abraham, 3 May 1908, Freud, 1965). He was in fact seeking two things. The first was a *scientific* foundation, indeed an *intellectual* basis of security, to enable him to grasp the dynamism of man's conscious and, in particular, his unconscious life; this he believed he had found in sexology (Freud, 1905) and, related to it, in drive theory (Freud, 1915). The second form of security he wanted would ensure the *survival* of the organization, practice, and science of psychoanalysis. Unable to establish this security in existing academic institutions, he was therefore forced to organize it himself, presumably on the model of the "-isms" that surrounded him in the political, artistic, and cultural life of his Viennese contemporaries (for example, Austro-Marxism, Zionism, nationalism, and Nazism on one hand, and positivism, empiriocriticism, expressionism, and all the other cultural "-isms" of the time, on the other).

He became the leader of this movement and may well have been embarrassed when Jones and Ferenczi suggested the formation of a secret committee (Jones to Freud, July 30, 1912, Freud, 1993): he did, after all, describe it as somewhat "infantile" (*knabenhaftes Element,* Freud to Jones, August 1, 1912). This embarrassment is perhaps to be seen as a premonition of something *unheimlich* (uncanny). He abandoned the known forms of scientific organization and even wondered whether it might not be a good plan for him and the psychoanalytic movement to join the Swiss apothecary Alfred Knapp's "International Order for an Ethic and a Culture," an enlightened, humanistic Free Mason–like movement that was spreading areligious and humanistic, ethical and cultural values.

Pushed by Ferenczi and Jones, he gave up these ideas and opted instead for an independent organization, implicitly keeping the values he had aimed at formerly. The outcome was to be the formation of the IPA and of the Secret Committee. (By the way, the Secret Committee, formed in 1912, was also supposed to control the then-president of the IPA, C. G. Jung, who completed his term by breaking with Freud in the same year.) The history of these two institutions has been written several times, and in critical, not just laudatory terms (Grosskurth, 1991; Leitner, 1998). A serious study of the psychoanalytic movement shows it to echo religion in its concepts of orthodoxy and heterodoxy, its expulsions reminiscent of the expulsion of Spinoza by the Jewish ecclesiastical authorities, and of the anathemas of the medieval Church, and even of confessions and reconversions. These last are illustrated by Otto Rank's famous circular letter of "repentance," in which he expressed his wish to present the explanation of his conduct to the members of the Secret Committee, "to apologize and finally make amends" (Lieberman, 1985, p. 248). Rank wrote that after "analytic interviews with Professor [Freud] Professor found my explanations satisfactory and forgave me personally" (p. 248). But only a few days later, he retracted his regretfulness—showing today's reader how difficult it was for him to stand up to his ego ideal, which incorporated an idealization of Freud. All these manifestations, at the limit of what is appropriate to a scientific movement, are ultimately seen to border on the temptation to become an exclusive and homogeneous fanatical group in possession of the one and only Truth. The issue is not whether Freud was right to protect his penetration into a difficult and uncertain field—the exploration of the unconscious—through his self-analysis and by all the interpretative methods that he himself sometimes described as "speculations" (Freud, 1900, p. 568; 1918, p. 206; 1920, p. 26; 1924, p. 177; 1930, p. 100). . . .

Yet our own means—those used by the majority of us—are not immune from the regressive wish to gain certainty by cutting the Gordian knot and setting ourselves up in a movement on the boundaries of fanaticism, *outside* the realm of intellectual dialogue, by isolating ourselves from the world in which we live, severing our contacts, and seeking security in this isolation in the name of loyalty to a tradition. Is our tradition close to the fanatical position, or do we, in fact, espouse pluralism and dialogue with the contemporary sciences—something that Freud always cultivated, for instance, with the neurological sciences, linguistics, anthropology, sexology, and endocrinology, and, more generally, representatives of the arts, such as poets, novelists, and other writers?

To reflect about fanaticism is not merely to think about our patients who are disgusted with sectarianism of all kinds and bring us wounds and depressions, and in some cases even nostalgia, after breaking with these "religions"; it also involves thinking about ourselves, with our yearning for intellectual and emotional security, which we cannot—because of our ideals!—allow ourselves to cultivate while we incline to maintain a fanatical position.

We must look at ourselves as potential fanatics. Our scientific position is not universally accepted; our scientific credibility and credentials are questioned. There are fanatics who interrogate us in a fanatic manner: "Freud bashing" speaks long lines about them. There may be economic reasons behind such Freud bashing (competition for the economic resources) and maybe envy and jealousy, and there also exist personally motivated remittances. But this is certainly not the whole story. On our side there is the attitude of promises overblown but not delivered, and uncertainty overcompensated by affirmations without sufficient proofs, as well as confusions between hypotheses and scientific truths: all these excesses are carried forward by our deep affective forces.

One of the phenomena we observe we could call a "group illusion" (Freud, 1921, p. 94). Behind it is revealed the ideal image invested in the leader: his way of thinking is so reassuring that it becomes a very important affective link for our scientific positions. Ernst Falzeder (1994) had the wonderful idea of showing how psychoanalytical groups and "schools" are constituted around a charismatic and reassuring figure with whom the group members conduct their training analysis ("family trees": see the Appendix that follows). In this way, the whole group was touched and profoundly influenced by the analyst. It suffices to analyze the bibliography of the psychoanalytical articles to discover that most of the citations are taken from the group of people to which the author belongs. For polemical reasons a few other thinkers are referred to, but they are apparently known more from hearsay than from close study or experience.

Intragroup communication and personal stimulation in these groups can be facilitated, so there is certainly a positive side. It is also undeniable, however, that the narcissistic confirmation of being an "insider" and object of mutual admiration, member of the most advanced group insofar as psychoanalytic knowledge is considered (the most scientific, for example), is a strong stabilizing factor. The organizational and political consequences can be drawn (see King and Steiner, 1991), and the passionate atmosphere created can be close to the limits of fanaticism. Fortunately this border is seldom trespassed, the paranoid projections and fears being kept under good control. Even so, the "group illusion" invested in the specific branch generates a considerable loss of information, interchange, and finally impoverishment. Here we are looking at the Freudian perspective directed at a complex group phenomenon that exists in lineages and the corresponding teachings of Freud and his successors.

In general, in struggling for understanding human nature, Freud teaches us to look first at ourselves. Wasn't *Gnothi Heauton*—look in the face of yourself—Freud's most important teaching?

REFERENCES

Bolterauer, L. (1975), Der Fanatismus. *Psyche,* 29:287–315.

Chasseguet-Smirgel, J. (1975), *L'Idéal du Moi.* Paris: Claude Tchou.

Chasseguet-Smirgel, J. & Grunberger, B. (1969), *L'Univers Contestationnaire.* Paris: Payot.

Falzeder, E. (1994), The threads of psychoanalytic filiations or psychoanalysis taking effect. In: *100 Years of Psychoanalysis,* ed. A. Haynal & E. Falzeder. Geneva: Cahiers Psychiatriques Genevois, pp. 176–181.

Freud, S. (1900), *The Interpretation of Dreams. Standard Edition,* 4–5. London: Hogarth Press, 1953.

Freud, S. (1905), *Three Essays on the Theory of Sexuality. Standard Edition,* 7:123–243. London: Hogarth Press, 1953.

Freud, S. (1915), *Instincts and Their Vicissitudes. Standard Edition,* 14:117–140. London: Hogarth Press, 1957.

Freud, S. (1918), *The Taboo of Virginity. Standard Edition,* 11:193–208. London: Hogarth Press, 1957.

Freud, S. (1920), *Beyond the Pleasure Principle. Standard Edition,* 18:7–64. London: Hogarth Press, 1955.

Freud, S. (1921), *Group Psychology and the Analysis of the Ego. Standard Edition,* 18:69–143. London: Hogarth Press, 1955.

Freud, S. (1924), *The Dissolution of the Oedipus Complex. Standard Edition,* 19:173–179. London: Hogarth Press, 1961.

Freud, S. (1927), *The Future of an Illusion. Standard Edition,* 21:5–56. London: Hogarth Press, 1959.

Freud, S. (1930), *Civilization and Its Discontents. Standard Edition,* 21:57–145. London: Hogarth Press, 1961.

Freud, S. (1965), *A Psycho-Analytic Dialogue: The Letters of Sigmund Freud and Karl Abraham 1907–1926.* London: Hogarth Press (New York: Basic Books, 1966).

Freud, S. (1993), *The Complete Correspondence of Sigmund Freud and Ernest Jones 1908–1939.* Cambridge, MA: Belknap Press.

Freud, S. (1996), *The Correspondence of Sigmund Freud and Sándor Ferenczi, Vol. 2, 1914–1919.* Cambridge, MA: Belknap Press.

Grosskurth, P. (1991), *The Secret Ring. Freud's Inner Circle and the Politics of Psycho-Analysis.* Reading, MA: Addison-Wesley.

Haldane, J. B. S. (1932), *The Inequality of Man and Other Essays.* Philadelphia: R. West.

King, P. & Steiner, R., eds. (1991), *The Freud–Klein Controversies 1941–45.* London: Routledge.

Koestler, A. (1978), *Janus: A Summing Up.* New York: Random House, 1979.

Lacan, J. (1956), Situation de la psychanalyse et formation du psychanalyste. In: *Ecrits.* Paris: Seuil, 1966, pp. 459–491.

Le Bon, G. (1895), *Psychologie des Foules.* Paris: Presses Universitaires de France, 1963.

Leitner, M. (1998), *Freud, Rank und die Folgen: Ein Schlüsselkonflikt für die Entwicklung der Psychotherapie des 20 Jahrhunderts.* Vienna: Turia & Kant.

Lieberman, E. J. (1985), *Acts of Will: The Life and Work of Otto Rank.* New York: The Free Press.

Pontalis, J. B. (1968), *Après Freud.* Paris: Gallimard.

Rangell, L. (1974), Psychoanalytic perspectives leading currently to the syndrome of the compromise of integrity. *Internat. J. Psycho-Anal.,* 55:3–12.

Reich, W. (1933), *The Mass Psychology of Fascism.* New York: Farrar, Straus & Giroux, 1970.

Steiner, G. (1981), *The Portage to San Cristobal of A. H.* London: Faber & Faber.

Vermorel, H. & Vermorel, M. (1993), *Sigmund Freud et Romain Rolland, Correspondance 1923–1936.* Paris: Presses Universitaires de France.

Weber, M. (1947), *The Theory of Social Economic Organization.* London: Oxford University Press.

APPENDIX

These "family trees" of early psychoanalysts and their analysands show how psychoanalytic groups and schools were constructed around charismatic or influential personalities. Figures 1 through 8 in this Appendix are from Falzeder (1994, pp. 176–181). Reproduced by permission.

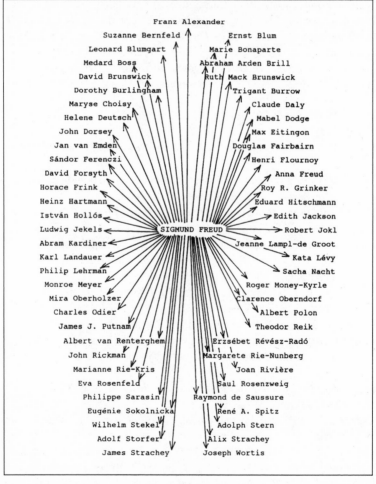

Figure 1

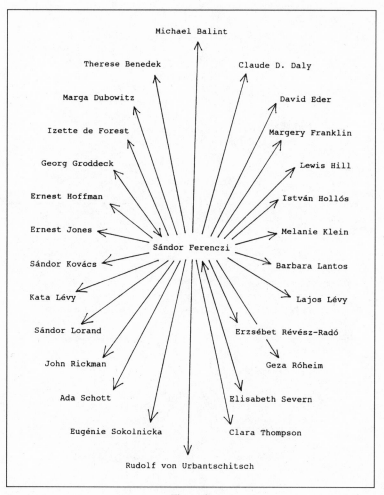

Figure 2

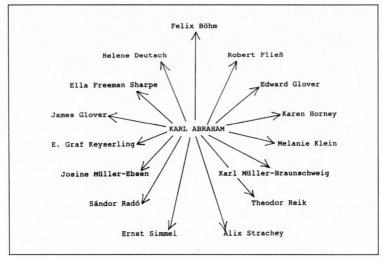

Figure 3

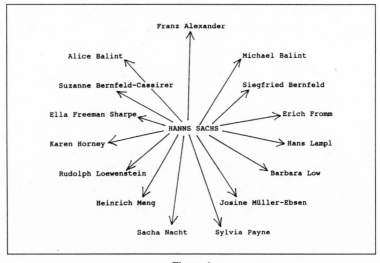

Figure 4

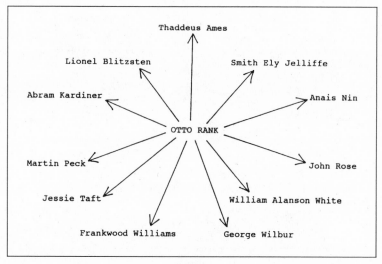

Figure 5

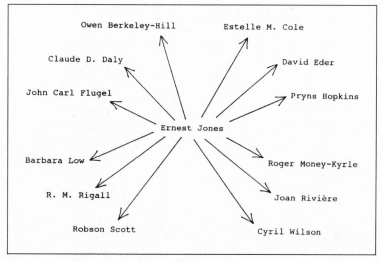

Figure 6

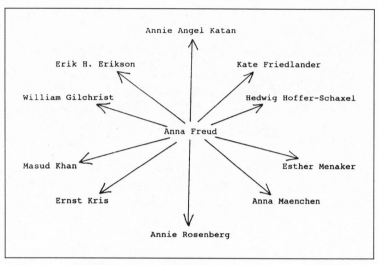

Figure 7

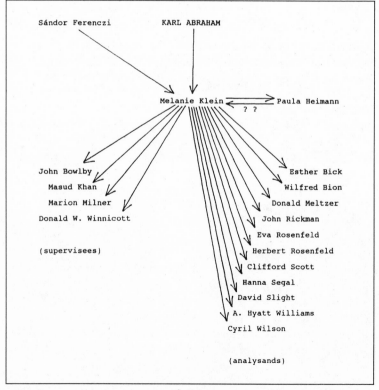

Figure 8

Group Psychology, Society, and Masses
Working with the Victims of Social Violence

YOLANDA GAMPEL

George Steiner (1999) defines a "classic" in literature, in music, and in philosophy as a signifier form that "reads" us. He claims that the classic "reads" us more than we read it. Each time we come in contact with a classic, it questions us and challenges our sources of consciousness and intelligence, of soul and body. A classic allows us to think and ask new questions; it allows for new thoughts to appear. The possibility for variation and mutation is infinite. This is the challenge when one is working on Freud's (1921) classic, *Group Psychology and the Analysis of the Ego*.

THE PLACE OF *GROUP PSYCHOLOGY* IN FREUD'S WRITINGS

After World War I, Freud wrote *The Uncanny* (1919) and *Beyond the Pleasure Principle* (1920). These books deal with the individual's facing the Uncanny, the dread and the compulsion to repeat, and the death drive. Freud presented both books as expansions of his previous ideas and theories, but we may wonder whether these works were not at least partly influenced by the war. The train of his own thinking and various world events may well have come together. Extraordinary events invariably alter our perception of reality. In a letter to Ferenczi, dated January 1919, Freud spoke of the war: "We devour each other" (Falzeder and Brabant, 1996).

The Uncanny, Freud's (1919) *Unheimlich,* is an unsettling experience: what is new and terrible presently becomes revealed as old and familiar. Conventional definitions of fright, dread, and horror are insufficient to encompass that "special core feeling" which makes *unheimlich* such a particular conceptual term. Freud explains that the uncanny represents something primary, already experienced, that was repressed. Without stating so explicitly, is not Freud also responding in *Group Psychology* to dreadful feelings arising from the social historical context (Verdun, the Armenian genocide), the uncanniness of World War I, and the dread and horror of social violence that belongs to the familiar, hidden and dangerous?

In *Beyond the Pleasure Principle* Freud (1920) considers the death drive. His preoccupation is without doubt related to the traumatic and posttraumatic reactions and consequences of World War I. Freud takes into account the biological and material roots of the death drive. From a biological standpoint, death destroys the bodily organization through decomposition. The unity of the individual is abolished. From an economic (psychological) point of view, there is an absolute dwindling of energy. Death is perceived as the result of an external destructor's operation. But the term death drive leads Freud to transpose the biological-somatic reference onto the organization of meanings and mental conflicts.

Freud is able to perceive death as an internal potentiality. Therefore, since death is considered to be internal, the control exerted over it is viewed as contingent on psychic reality. It follows that there is a coexistence of opposites in psychic reality; internal and external, self in closure that hurts and sometimes leads to psychic death, and the diffusion of violence into the world.

Another opposition may be found between overfullness and complete emptiness, which leads to possible destruction resulting from any of the following antinomies: control or the lack of it; rigid fusion or fragmentation, rejection of mirroring or rejection of the other, the *Heimlich* or the *Unheimlich.*

In psychic reality, how is death represented? The nullification of all tensions that hold structures and consciousness, which become permanent and irreversible, is a mental representation of death. It is as if a form of fantasy were required to defeat death. Therefore, poets have sought lyric equivalences: sexuality, orgasm, sleep are invoked to represent death.

Death is thus at least ostensibly conquered and granted beneficial value. We also find nirvana in the quest to abolish all tensions, a quest manifested in oriental thought. Nirvana is unique in that it is an acquired serenity allowing for sidetracking the will to live, death being perceived through adhesion to life. Another way to view death is through the breaking of links, the fragmentation found in psychosis, which may be considered equivalent to a kind of mental death.

In his third work, *Group Psychology,* written after World War I, Freud enters the field of social psychology; he explores the connection between power and the manipulation of masses; and, referring both to natural and to artificial groups, he tells the history of the individual and of society. As one rereads his work, the question that comes to mind is, how would Freud have written this book after World War II? What form would his theories concerning the death drive and mass psychology have taken after Auschwitz and Hiroshima?

Freud anticipated in his *Group Psychology* the rise of the uncivilized mob, whose attachment to a powerful leader embodying a group's feelings and values could provide compensatory modes of behavior and unreflective social action. In chapter five of his essay, Freud displays a simultaneously optimistic and pessimistic view about the mass movements in the world:

> If today that intolerance no longer shows itself so violent and cruel as in former centuries, we can scarcely conclude that there has been a softening in human manners. The cause is rather to be found in the undeniable weakening of religious feelings and the libidinal ties which depend upon them. If another group tie takes the place of the religious one—and the socialistic tie seems to be succeeding in doing so—then there will be the same intolerance towards the outsiders as in the age of the Wars of Religion; and if differences between scientific opinions could ever attain a similar significance for groups, the same result would again be repeated with this new motivation [p. 128].

MASS AND SOCIETY IN OUR TIME: MASS–CROWD–MOB 1921–1999

Freud (1921) defines mass psychology as the simultaneous influence on an individual by a large number of people who are strangers to him: "Mass psychology is therefore concerned with the individual man as a member of a race, of a nation, of a caste, of a profession, of an institution, or as a component part of a crowd of people who have been organized into a mass at some particular time for some definite purpose" (p. 70).

In order to imagine ourselves as a mass we need to evoke the feeling of being in a crowd and our double perception of ourselves in it, where we simultaneously feel both the attraction and the fear of being assimilated or lost in the crowd. Freud, through Le Bon, describes a mass as a "living crowd" in need of a sense of safety and looking up to its leader for an ego ideal. In our mass society, we are not persons in a crowd but, rather, elements in the inert mass program of statistics and computers, "inert identities," in which the definition of ourselves as "wholes" is determined by unknown others. In this way, statistics come to command the collective unconscious, dictating values of different kinds in which we are trapped. Some would assert, subtly, that the world today offers more possibilities to be treated as a thing than as a person (Amati Sas and Gampel, 1997).

Now, in retrospect, we view genocide and the unraveling of the vicissitudes of both communism and capitalism, people having paid the price for the intolerance of dogmatic thinking on both sides. At present we are witnessing the resurgence of religious extremism. In addition, science is providing more means for destruction, and we can indeed quote Freud (1921) once more, "the same result would again be repeated with the same motivation" (p. 100). But our world is quite different from Freud's. In our era, we see, on one hand, the development of the concept of "globalization," a phenomenon of unification and homogenization in which economy and technology are regrouped in enterprises functioning globally. Globalized capital creates a new transnational class of elites, linked by satellites. New modes of communication allow for new kinds of closeness, and images of information circulate at high speed within global consumer culture. But, on the other hand, we are subject to, as well as the observers of, a confusion between mass psychology and individual psychology. We perceive only parts of this phenomenon and lack an organizing principle that would allow us to give meaning to these dispersions. Instead, we invoke clichés to give meaning to this reality. We then face an interruption in the dialectic between identity and alterity, which, according to Durkheim (1925), catalyzes the appearance of signs of violence. Production and consumership are a mass-mediated popular culture valorizing privatized hedonism.

The newly arisen phenomena of the media and of the image, which affect communication, are changes that are represented as cultures. We also come to view religious movements as creating a present identity through rituals. The history of our times lies somewhere between the image of historical-religious myth, through which new revelations are sought, and the image presented by the media, which preserves, almost automatically, the myth of modern life. It is life between the illusion-hallucination of the past, and the illusion-hallucination of the present and the future. Kernberg (1998) defines mass culture as "those forms of cultural expression that appeal to individuals under conditions in which they are influenced by real or fantasized masses" (p. 254). He views mass culture as cultivated by means of communication, namely, the press, radio, cinema, and television.

The visual is a world of immediacy—no frustration. The visual is the typical form of the dream and primary process; visual images evoke feelings of love, fear, joy, anxiety, anger. But mass media, and especially television, do not provide to the individual any double-perception of being in a crowd, which is precisely the feeling that allows the individual to defend himself once inside a crowd. Our transsubjective participation in mass media is far less evident: we are touched, led, penetrated by images, with little or no possibility for defense, since it is easier to accept the offered reality without conflict and to take it for granted. Of course, we try to interpret reality, to detect causality, to comprehend events, but we do not perceive our being treated as a mass. The lack of awareness of the manner in which one is treated by others constitutes the definition of alienation. We defend ourselves through adaptation by becoming conformist and, somehow, ambiguous (Amati Sas, 1992), as we accept without conflict the many inert identifications foisted on us.

Statistics and computers contribute to this state of affairs. Through the media, human beings can dispose of others' psychic realities, but the "megamachine culture" (Amati Sas, 1985) imposes its values on them as well. The modes of communication and imagery techniques turn relations with the other into an abstraction; we are used to seeing everything, but are we looking? On the other hand, we witness the fall of confederations and the momentary need for the recognition of singularity, particularity, religious difference and ethnicity, which are invoked with force and sometimes lead to breakpoints and murderous violence.

In our Western culture, we could very generally claim that racism is the collective parallel to individual narcissism, that is, a nonacceptance of the difference of the other and a rejection of the similarities between the in-group and the other. A narcissist wishes that others were similar to him, but forbids it, concomitantly barring any possibility for community. Violence appears here, and it is continually replayed in a vicious circle. The protection of all identity, in the form forged by narcissism when it becomes linked to territorial protection, mobilizes violence into action. The need to protect identity and territory simultaneously presupposes a large variety of potential reactions determined by cultural, educational, and parental ideals. One consequence is migration, which is explained by unequal economic circumstances in different areas of the world; another consequence is outright expulsion, that is, millions of people being expelled from their countries owing to political circumstances, fleeing, and seeking refuge without having a place to harbor.

THE EXPANSION OF OUR UNDERSTANDING OF GROUPS

For Sartre (1960), alienation is part of human existence. From the moment one is born, one is alienated and must struggle against alienation. The two primary forms of alienation are otherness and objectification. When it is possible to surmount being only one among many, a relation of reciprocity may be achieved denoting that each is for the other what he is to himself ("Thou shalt love thy neighbor as thyself"). There is an internalization of the other as a human link. Sartre's notions of seriality (one among many) and alienation lead us to conclude that our need for communication is a means of defense against chaos and massification. The experience of chaos in a group is related to the impossibility of finding minimal forms of linkage; it connects the individual with solitude and anomie. The defense against anxiety is the adhesion to stereotyped, strict rules. The experience of massification in a group is like the loss of the individual ego and a search for an ideal, illusory, group ego. There is no longer a "we" but, rather, "the group." In this process of massification, communication is interrupted because of a loss of differentiation between self and other.

Sartre asserts that the group constitutes itself as an attempt to struggle against alienation and seriality. All members unite against a common danger. In its development, the group nourishes itself from situations it must overcome. For Sartre, seriality is a type of human relation in which each member can be substituted by an undifferentiated other. This means attributing to the human being the characteristic of a thing, so that the only possible existence of a group is in the form of a series of alienated individuals. This joint experience of seriality may also be the starting point of each group or mass movement.

Bleger (1967), following Freud, showed that, even in cases that seem to present themselves as a seriality, what seems to appear as a state of no-relation, there exists an unconscious and syncretic relation between the individual psyche and those of others. Bleger believes in the following idea: that individual identity will form itself on the basis of group-related and mutual indifference.

Bion (1970) wrote about groups from the standpoint of an analyst who had exposed himself to the emotional turmoil of becoming a member of the group, whereas Freud wrote about group phenomena from a distance. Bion stated that the group needs a mystic, a "continued supply of genius." But the group must remain vital and grow. The mystic needs the group to provide the conditions in which his genius can thrive and grow, but the relation between them is always problematic; the mystic is disruptive to the group, challenging its existing state and coherence and seemingly threatening the group with catastrophe. These threats cause tensions and drives that are directed toward the destruction of the mystic and the preservation of the group and its coherence, even at the cost of stunting growth and vitality.

Here we confront the problem of disidentification from the mystic. Bion's (1961) fundamental concepts of the basic assumption group, as distinguished from the work group, differentiate the irrational aspect of the group from its rational aspect and make a distinction between a regressed and a more mature-functioning group. We can see this distinction in the differentiation between the description of Le Bon's (1895) and McDougall's (1920) groups. Bion, however, emphasizes that, in every group, one aspect of the group rests on a basic assumption. The only question is whether the basic assumption function is in the service of the work group or whether the assumption runs away with the group.

The major question that Freud posed, as did Bion, is how to make the dark, irrational, primitive forces in man manageable. Freud called them drives, whereas Bion managed the problem by assuming a double-aspect in man, especially the man-in-a-group: the rational/scientific and the irrational/primitive, lost in fantasy. The difference between Freud's and Bion's thinking also lies in how each views the emotional experience: how human beings seek to avoid or attain certain emotional experiences above and beyond mere gratification and discharge.

Pichon-Riviere (1975) formulated the notion of the link, which he defined as a complex structure that includes the subject, the object, and their mutual interrelations with learning and communication processes. This learning process will be facilitated or obstructed depending on the dialectic or dilemmatic (antagonistic) confrontation between the realms of intersubjective and intrasubjective. This means that the process of identification will function like an open circuit leading to a spiral trajectory or like a stereotyped closed system. Pichon-Riviere viewed the internal world as a system that includes the interaction of relational objects in mutual renourishment while simultaneously maintaining interaction with the environment. The substitution of the notion of the drive by the link structure necessitates defining psychology as social psychology. Pichon-Riviere submitted that all his suggestions were the consequence of a praxis and could be found in Freud's work—especially in *Group Psychology*—but that this formulation implied a break from orthodox psychoanalytical thought.

Berenstein and Puget (1997) provide a metapsychological amplification of this notion. Their conception holds that the link is a basic construct for the creation of subjectivity, which inhabits three independent spaces simultaneously, each with its specific representations. This conceptualization is very different from the object relationship, which is intrasubjective. These theoreticians propose a bipolar unconscious organization (two egos, described as virtual observers, or one ego and another seen from within the self, with an intermediary connecting them).

INTERRELATION BETWEEN MAN AND SOCIETY

In *Group Psychology and the Analysis of the Ego,* Freud (1921) tries to deal with the ways in which internal psychic reality and external reality are interrelated and influenced by one another, concomitantly, synchronically and diachronically, and whether this process takes place in accordance with the logic of the unconscious or that of the conscious. In the entire body of his work, this is where he comes closest to describing the inner world. He begins with a very decisive assertion: "In the individual's mental life someone else is invariably involved, as a model, as an object, as a helper, as an opponent and so from the very first individual psychology, in this extended but entirely justifiable sense of the words, is at the same time social psychology as well" (p. 68).

Freud then refers to the human being's relations to parents, brothers and sisters, object of love, the doctor. These relations have all been studied by psychoanalysis and may be considered as social phenomena. These phenomena might stand in opposition to narcissistic phenomena, but we can observe, on the basis of Melanie Klein's contribution to psychoanalysis, that narcissism is also related to external links that have been internalized, that is, relations that we call "internal links," which are reproduced within the space of the ego as a form of group relations. These structures of links, which include the subject, the object, and the interrelation, are configured by extremely early experiences.

Freud insists on the need to differentiate between groups but affirms that the interrelation between individuals always exists and that the stipulation of a primary social drive (the social instinct, the "herd instinct," the "group mind") is not necessary to account for this interrelation. This means that an individual can become a human being only by leaning on the social sphere. It is only the other who is able to recognize the individual and grant him a place within the social sphere, however it is symbolized. It follows that the other is always present within the self, through the mechanism of incorporation or internalization, both of which allow for identification. Simultaneously, the other, who is so important to the creation of the psyche, cannot completely determine the individual's behavior, as it always remains partially autonomous and original to the self. The collection of internalized relations, which are in permanent interaction and activation, constitutes the internal group with accompanying relations and unconscious fantasy.

Psychoanalytic attention focuses on the membrane that differentiates the world from ourselves. This idea of such a membrane allowed Anzieu (1985) to work through, on the basis of contributions of Esther Bick (1968, 1984), John Bowlby (1973), Wilfred Bion (1962), and D. W. Winnicott (1988), the concept of "ego skin." When referring to identification, we presuppose the existence of a relation with a separated object; the formation of the ego depends on the manner in which the real mother holds and handles the baby (Winnicott, 1965) and contains him (Bion, 1962). Anzieu depicts the ego skin as a figuration that the child's ego uses during the first phases of development to represent himself as an ego through his experience with his body. This ego skin functions simultaneously as a sack that retains in the good and the sensation of plenty, as a protective barrier, and as a place and a means for the first exchange with the other (Anzieu, 1985).

Prior to the onset of the process of identification, which requires a relation to an object, and prior to the existence of a group or society, we can see the importance for the definition of what constitutes the child himself of the presence of a membrane that retains and protects, while also allowing the first relation to an other. First relying on bodily functions, an individual comes to depend on other persons and groups, with the human psyche structuring itself progressively in a movement of leaning/ loss/return to transformative, creative leaning. The human being moves between leaning on narcissistic objects, which reinforce closure, and choosing objects to lean on which allow for a meeting with the other and ultimately allow for creativity.

IDENTIFICATION

The concept of identification is central to the understanding of the organization and development of the personality in relation to the external world, and it is central, as well, to *Group Psychology:* "and so from the very first individual psychology, is at the same time social psychology as well" (p. 68). This concept is fundamental to our understanding of the development of the ego, the superego, the ego ideal, character, and identity. It is a constant in the continuous interchange between subject and object. As Freud states, the first behavior of a child toward his object of desire is to his wish to swallow it, to consume it, and to recreate it within his own ego. This is the basis of identification. If we think of identification as part of every interpersonal relationship, we can see that it creates a current of sympathy between the individual and the object, not only because they will then share similar attitudes and emotions, but because it allows one to put oneself into the place of the other, to understand his thinking and behavior. We have to distinguish identification from imitation. Freud discusses this issue in *Group Psychology* through the three concepts of suggestion, contagion, and fascination. Identification is an unconscious mechanism that produces modifications in the subject, while imitation is a reactive reproduction of certain acts. Both processes may be integrated. Freud proposes various types of identification, but he recognizes only three sources: the first is identification, the most primitive form of tie with an object; the second identification replaces the tie with the object and introjects it regressively into the ego; and the third type of identification may arise with any new perception of a common quality shared with some other person who is not an object of sexual desire.

Identification in the group is based on an important common emotional quality. Freud (1921) compares identification with falling in love and discusses the problem of group formation. In the case of falling in love, the ego is enriched by acquiring qualities that are admired in the object, but, at the same time, the ego is impoverished because it submits to the object, which takes the place of the ideal of the ego. And so, from falling in love to hypnosis, there is but one step to be taken. A primary group is an amalgam of individuals who have put the same object in place of their egos' ideals; consequently, they each identify with the others. In some way we can refer to this phenomenon as very similar to narcissistic identification, described by Esther Bick (1984) as "adhesive identification." As its name implies, it is a singular form of identification, superficial and empty, without consistency or depth, mere skin-to-skin contact. Adhesive identification seems to produce a type of clinging dependence, in which the separate existence of the object is unrecognized. It is similar to the mass phenomenon described by Freud, referring to Le Bon (1895), in which an individual's laws lose their separate existence as the leader figures are taken absolutely for granted, in the same way as one generally takes the obedience of one's hand to one's intentions for granted.

Freud describes the collapse that results when in such situations there is a rejection of dependency, because the feeling is that of being torn off and thrown away by the object-leader. We can therefore detect the entry point where narcissistic identification becomes projective identification. Projective identification involves confusion, when something that belongs to the subject is passed into the object, resulting in the former's losing his individuality, while the latter is invested with what, in fact, does not belong to him. It involves a subject and identity that are alien to him to blur his image and superimpose him onto the other. This process is described very well by Le Bon in his discussion of mass phenomena and by Freud (1921) when he explains the emotional themes of hordes and mobs, the sense of closeness, and their impulsive behavior, all deriving from the projection of their ego ideal onto the leader, and their identification with the leader as well as with each other.

THE VICISSITUDES OF IDENTIFICATION AFTER THE SHOAH

The world has much changed since the horrors that culminated in the Shoah. The totalitarian states of the 30s have crumbled. But nationalism, racism and hatred are still with us. The forms of identification that Freud described in *Group Psychology* and in other writings were based on his clinical experience with hysterics who suffered somatic conversions. But post-WWII, conceptualization of identification was put forward through formulations of more impulse-driven character disorders, described as narcissistic, borderline, and self-related pathologies.

Since World War II and especially following Auschwitz and Hiroshima, we are faced with treating patients who went through extreme situations of social violence. This clinical experience has brought about new formulations of increasingly extreme concepts, using extreme wording. For example, Puget (1991), elaborating on Freud's ideas, takes into account social violence through the introduction of the unthinkable and the unthought. The acceptance of this category is for Puget "equivalent to tolerating the existence of an unknowable mental space whose transformation into words would produce madness and death. It also means tolerating the existence of a world outside the ego, in which the subject is immersed but without being able to know that this is so. It also suggests recognition of the unknowable-unshareable, of sensory knowledge" (p. 123).

Wilgowicz (1999), discussing the repercussions of the Nazi genocide of the Jews on the descendants of victims and survivors, conceptualizes a typical vampiric form of identification in which the subject is stated to be neither dead nor alive, unborn, in an imageless, timeless, and spaceless condition, imprisoned in an earlier generation's traumas. The author asserts that analysis in such cases must tackle the genocide-induced fantasies of a vampire complex involving infanticide and parricide in addition to the incestuous and parricidal wishes stemming from the Oedipus complex.

I (Gampel, 1996) liken the sort of identification found in Shoah survivors to radiation: an external reality enters the psychic apparatus without the individual's having any control over its entry, implantation, and effects. This "radioactive identification" (Gampel, 1999) comprises nonrepresentable remnants, remainders of the radioactive influences of the external world that are imbedded within the individual. These influences affect and lead to a reverberation in different institutions, large groups, and nations and come back to the individual through transgenerational transmission. If we agree that we are the children of our times, then we may look at our time as reflecting the cruelty of our era and therefore should also expect that this engraved evidence will be reflected by depositing its radioactive experiences into us. As I explore here, the effects of these remnants often will be expressed in future generations.

What is it that awaits us in the 21st century with regard to the conceptualizations that describe the soul's state as it fragments into innumerable pieces owing to the effects of social violence? Can psychoanalysis do anything more than just cure the wounds? Can we prevent anything?

RADIOACTIVE IDENTIFICATION

I suggest a concept that can express the influence on the individual and further generations of the massive impact of social violence (Gampel, 1993, 1996, 1999). This is what occurs when the individual is considered but a thing in a mass, when the impact of the external world touches all the personality's dimensions and penetrates them like radium. This radiation, penetrating all levels of the subject, leads to a specific kind of identification.

To restate my concept of "radioactivity": an external reality enters the psychic apparatus without the individual's having any control over its entry, implantation, or effects. The concept of radioactive identification is a conceptual and metaphoric representation of the penetrations of the terrible, violent, and destructive aspects of external reality against which the individual is defenseless. This radioactive identification, or "radioactive nucleus," comprises nonrepresentable remnants, remainders of the radio-active influences of the external world, which are embedded within the individual. These nonrepresentable remnants of the radioactive influence cannot be spoken about or described in words. They reveal themselves through images, symptoms, and dreams.

The individual internalizes the radioactive remnants, of which he is unaware, and identifies with them and their dehumanizing aspects. He later acts out these identifications, which are alien to him, or otherwise they are acted out by his children through the process of transgenerational transmission.

One can speculate that the perception of violence has, like radioactivity, infiltrated and made its way into the three spaces of the psyche, thus contaminating them (Berenstein and Puget, 1997). Each space will accept or reject this radioactivity according to its own particular rules of functioning. The role of psychoanalysis in this regard is to enable us to work through the unsavory aspects of our own psychic involvement in the collective trauma. Thus, we may be able to find the golden mean between over-and underestimation of our role in the social context (Gampel, 1992).

The problem is the way in which violent, aggressive sadism leads to the erasure of boundaries and causes the infusion of the individual into the mass. It is important that we all experience ourselves as persons, while being part of the collective, as well; we each must remain singular, one, refinding the dimension of humanity as against the mass and mass crimes. The attack against that which was human during the Shoah affected not only life, but also death, which was reduced to the status of an object, devoid of heuristic value (Moscovitz, 1998). Attacking death by objecti-fying it meant the rupture of history, because the origins of history were based on the possibility of narrating the death of people who had lived. If we cannot tell the story because the disappearance itself has been erased, then death cannot become historic. The story cannot be written, and it is given the status of a divisible, concrete object.

In Freud's text, which we have just finished reviewing in the light of those points that were evocative for us, psychic reality includes a histori-cal-cultural inheritance that is common to both psychoanalyst and patient. I suggest that the traces of social violence should be taken into account. Failure to "read" or acknowledge these traces in clinical material will affect future psychic possibilities. Auschwitz and Hiroshima are our common background and legacy in this century (Gampel, 1997).

A REFLECTIVE GROUP WITH
VICTIMS OF SOCIAL VIOLENCE

Finally, I would like to acquaint you with a very special experience with a group of people that in some ways exemplifies some of the issues dealt with here. The group was composed of people who had gone through the terrible and traumatic experience of social violence during the 20th century, the Shoah. The group met regularly over a period of seven years, with the goal in mind of thinking and reflecting together on the participants' pasts and present lives. The group met on a fixed day once a month for three-hour encounters; this was an open group in which people who had been previously interviewed were invited to take part. Some 30 to 40 people participated in the encounters (Gampel, 1998). The encounter from which the following excerpts were taken was held on July 2, 1990; this was the last encounter before the summer break. The group's situation allowed the emergence of material, processes, and conscious and unconscious configurations otherwise inaccessible. This group encounter vividly illustrates the inscription of massive social violence and the possibilities that exist for working with the trauma and finding the space for healing and recuperation. These excerpts are parts of the conversation in the group, selected to illustrate the ideas just presented. The order of citations does not correspond to the order of the original meeting but is organized according to themes. Contents, however, have been only minimally changed or edited. The speaker's gender is clear from each citation.

The Group Deals with the Theme of the
Uncanny That Emerges

Group members try to avoid a return to and experience of violence in their *intrasubjective worlds* as well as in the *intersubjective world,* to figure out how to avoid generating more violence:

One of the participants:

Mr. B: Within myself I found out that, really, my situation is good. My situation is excellent! I tried to recapitulate that to myself. It could be that I was a young child, even very young, maybe too young. My terrible experiences of the Holocaust, well, I was 7 or 8 years old when I went through that, and maybe I was fortunate, because I was young enough to be able to put things so deep in the back of my consciousness that I can do pretty well in life, and I can also look at the bright side and hope for a better tomorrow [taking a breath]. And this brings me to this conflict we had here in the last encounter. It's quite clear that I can't just stand there quietly when someone comes and tries to tell me that "life is all black." I can't have anyone tell me that "there are no blue skies, the sky is black, the sun is the same sun." I find this infuriating. Nothing changed. This is why I was so upset about these things. I wasn't so angry when someone tried to analyze every movement and every step, but to tell me such things!

Another group member:

Mr. C: I want to tell you, man! You went through the Holocaust when you were very young, you say you were 7 or 8. There are older people here, like me, when I went through the Holocaust I was 20. The older the person is, it makes the Holocaust he went through blacker.

Mr. B: Never, not 20 years ago, not 70 years ago, . . . my children never knew anything about us. Not a word. My wife went through Holocaust, and I went through Holocaust. We never spoke about it. It was taboo. Now, too, we don't speak about it, but they ask and we answer. That's all we do.

Mrs. D: Why is it happening? Now I find myself imagining—I, who lost my whole family! I find myself imagining in what way they finished them, and I know how they finished them. It comes to me every night, not in dreams, but when I'm awake, with my eyes closed. And every year it's getting worse, the pictures I imagine, and I didn't actually see how. So the question is, why is this so? It's a world of the past, and I already went through that and I have a new life and it's all very nice and well, and I went to Hungary and back. With my Israeli passport, I was one of those who were really happy for being an Israeli when I returned to Hungary. I went there several times and really enjoyed it very much. I went to, and returned from, that special place where I vowed that my children, if I was ever to get away from that hell, that my children would be born there . . . my daughter, my granddaughter. I met them, that is, I took them to that place where I had made that vow. What I mean is that my children were born here, and my granddaughter. And it was really great, until a few weeks ago that the thing with the newspapers started. I, who buy every day almost all the newspapers, started noticing that I was trying to find myself in a situation, that is, as if not on purpose, in which I do not buy the newspaper. [She is referring to the Intifada.]

[Y.G. (the coordinator of the group): It sounds as if they feel that "The State of Israel," as a protective envelope, is failing them.]

Mrs. D: Now I'm full of anxiety, anxiety—what's going to happen? With my children, and what's going to happen to my grandchildren, if what happened to us should happen to you? We live in a country, our country, and in the past it was only me and my strength.

Mrs. Z: My anxieties did not only come from the outside world, but also from the internal changes I experienced, the age, the children having grown up, that all of a sudden people close to me started to die on me . . . and I felt thrown back precisely to that period of losing people one after the other, one by one. The children are grown up now. They don't need me . . . and I never really asked myself truthfully who it was to whom I owed this being such a good mother. I always say that I fought Hitler and won, by proving to him that I could raise children like you said: children who excelled. Sadly, but excelling in many fields and disciplines. And they're humane human beings, too. To me, this was the most important.

From Guilt and Shame for Surviving to Pride over Survival, from Helplessness During the Shoah to a Will to Struggle

Mrs. M: And when I came to the group I found out that, apart from the fact that we were all children in the Holocaust, some were older, some were younger. I think that Mrs. Z was among the very young. I was very young when the Holocaust started. I was barely four. And all of a sudden I was filled with such a pride. I was only a four-year-old girl, who fought six years to survive. At four-and-a-half I was already an orphan, and I fought and managed to survive without anybody in particular being in charge of taking care of me. Those things I was so ashamed of—that I was an orphan and that I was raised, after the war, by a foster caretaker. All of a sudden, with the help of the group, all these things became something I can be proud of. This is something I would never have thought of on my own. Another thing that comes to my mind is, well it's not meant as an insult but as a compliment: how egocentric we are, how much we all see all the time those things that happened to us, which become like a circle around us. And it's not . . . well, in the end, its a very open type of egocentricity. Because we are very willing to accept criticism, comments.

The third thing is the will, which I said I felt as an individual, but I can see it as very characteristic of the whole group. is the will to win. There's no other name for it because, if there is, then why do we keep saying that we survived, or have overcome? We fought, we struggled, we coped with our fears and anxieties. It's not that we suppressed them and buried them. We overcame our anxieties, and moreover, at home we fought to raise our children well. What makes us really proud when we look at our next generation? It's true that we demanded a lot from them. Anyway, I admit today that what I thought to be very legitimate, well, maybe I demanded too much, but I demanded, I had expectations, I knew how to demand, and now we have children who are successful. This is my impression of all of us.

From Being Helped and Contained to the Provision of Containment and Help

Mrs. D: I'll try to start from the beginning of that year. Tammy gave me the script, the transcription of these encounters. An encounter between people who were children during the Holocaust, how they are dealing and coping with life, how they live this in a perspective of the present and the future. Maybe this was what I meant, what I attuned myself to.

Mr. F: During the year there were several meetings which were really very much to the point, meetings that did something to the soul inside. This was for me the first time I could see myself in the feelings of other people. This was the first time I met something which I didn't know existed in me, and here, all of a sudden you can see it around the table, out in the open. There were times when this caused closed things, those shut drawers, those hidden things to want to emerge and peep out. In fact, there is no doubt in my mind that, having faced the fact that there are actually people who, to my great surprise, feel very much like I do, have the same doubts, the things they don't understand are the same things that I don't understand, and they look for the same things I look for. Well, that's really something. That really did something to me. It allowed me to analyze, to open things up, to summarize things for myself, to see things in an entirely new light.

Second Generation

One of the survivors' children present at the meeting confronted the group with her culture as a child of a survivor. She expressed her struggle to break free from the transmitted radioactive identification.

What bothered me most in what she said, is that you said, I was really moved by the way you described everything. But what I found very hard was that you said "I too had excellent children, my children are excelling, too, and they are human beings, too. And I was also strong and my children are strong" and all that. I can't stand it anymore. That's precisely what makes me suffer, what pains me, and I just can't stand it anymore. I can't stand being excellent anymore, I can't stand being so strong and such a heroine anymore. And I don't want to succeed as much as my mother wants to . . . she wants to pass it on to her children. This is what she had children for, so they could survive like she did. Incidentally, today I thought of this. I spoke about this with someone. I'm 26 and all I do is survive.

I don't live, I only survive. [Audience: What's she talking about?] I feel I survive, I fight every day, all the time for what I feel, what I need to achieve, what people expect from me.

But I don't have to survive, I'm not going through any war. I need to live and enjoy, and achieve—or not—and to fail and to be strong or weak. And that's what I got, of course, unintentionally, all out of good will, without any bad intentions. But this is what I've been through. With all the best intentions of so many parents who went through the Holocaust, who wanted to make their children strong against all the problems, and they transmitted to them this strong feeling that you have to fight for everything, that you have to be a hero, that you have to be strong. [Audience: Consciously or unconsciously?] Unconsciously, of course it's unconscious. [Audience: You're wrong, it's just not true what you are saying.] I didn't say that everyone's like that, I'm not speaking of others, I'm speaking of myself. I feel I received from my mother the ability to survive, which is a great thing, but do I need to fight for survival? No, I don't. But I did receive it, and really, I'm very successful.

Mrs. A: I wanted to say that I came here, and that for many years these things were hidden very deep inside me. I don't know if it was taboo or not. Anyway, I never spoke about it. Here, it's the first time ever that I opened my heart, here I found a place where I can speak, freely, about the things that happened to me. And I'm not the only one, I have more partners to this story. I'm not exceptional. [Responses from the audience: But on the outside you still keep silent?] Outside, no one wants to hear me anymore. They hush me up. But here I opened up, something that was buried down deep for many many years . . . when they caught Eichmann, or when there was the Demyaniuk trial, well, even then I didn't speak so much. But here, it was the first time I opened up.

Second-generation participant, *Mrs. W:* When I spoke of survival, I spoke exactly of what my mother speaks of, and this is precisely where I see my difficulty is. The fact that I have to tell the truth no matter what, because that's what she passed on to me, this is my war. Because I'm not allowed to miss anything, or to tell anything but the total truth. And when I need to feel free to feel the way I feel, then I fight over it no matter what, with everyone. I always tell everyone: "I have the right to feel the way I feel!" And everyone says, "What does she want with me? Of course, she has the right to feel like that." But I still have to fight over everything. Those things which were so important to her, which she fussed about, are now equally important to me and I fuss about them, and it's not natural, I'm only 26 and like a five-year-old girl. I don't have to tell the truth no matter what, I'm allowed to lie, and I'm allowed to do lots of things.

Mrs. E: I also went through a lot. I went through Bergen Belzen and lots of camps. And, as for the children, it's true. This is how my children felt. I never spoke at home, but that's how they felt.

I was a 13-year-old girl when the war started. I was left alone. So what did I know about raising children? I thought: "If she doesn't eat, she'll die on me." And there's another thing, which even today I dream about, I don't dream that *I'm* running away as a child, that I'm scared, but that I'm fleeing *with* them, with *my* children [her voice cracks] . . . I feel them, still . . . It's my whole life. And I really don't want to think about it so much. I always reject it and avoid it but it comes back to me during the night.

The Group Begins to Deal with
What Is Currently Happening in Israel at the Time,
Namely, the Palestinian Uprising,
Also Known as the Intifada

A question from the audience: How do you get along with this spring of hatred?

Mr. S: It's not a spring of hatred. I still haven't left Auschwitz. [Everyone: Uh-hmm.] I still see the burning crematoriums, I see our children, I see how they collected the bags full of babies in the camp, in the Lodz ghetto, and threw them down. I see a Hitler-Jugend practicing his shooting and how they told the children to run.

Seventy thousand Jews, for three days, the Germans herded them and led them to Auschwitz and burned them. Only a handful of them remained, so is this something you can forget? [Voices from the audience: Who's forgetting? No one's forgetting. What do you think we come here for?] The question is, do we want to kill and run others down? The question is, do I want to see my kid killing all the time and running others down, in order to remain standing, a hero?

It's a question of survival. He who wants to kill you—kill him first! That's life's motto.

Such a group, constituted by members who have suffered social violence and who share a common background and life history (e.g., surviving the Holocaust as children or adolescents), should be regarded as a sort of "ethnic community." Such groups may present typical problems, which we have to take into consideration in our work with them: The symbolic and imaginary may become homogeneous but have no common denominator; they become a group according to the others' point of view of them; they come together not because of love, but, rather, because of anger and hatred toward the others, who do not know how to accept them. Their desire is to "disidentify," to search for other forms of identification, which will allow them to belong to the culture.

What happened with this group? The group provided survivors with a space in which to think together about their pasts, their loved ones, their traumas, and their feelings of guilt and shame. It provided perspectives on memories, which worked themselves back and forth between remembering and being conscious of a specific memory, between the narration of an event and the need to understand it and give it meaning, between an event's description and its profound analysis and interpretation.

A new solidarity formed that stemmed from the shared suffering. It enabled group members to establish a new rapport with their bodies, their uniqueness, their individual histories, their present, and their future, and with their fellow survivors. Through the group, survivors could project the clarity of systematic thinking onto the concentration camp system and reacquire the sense of efficacious struggle.

From the participants' statements following several years of work together we can relate to the differences between testimony, evacuation, association in the here-and-now, and thinking together about extreme situations. Representing the interminable working through and interrelations among mass, mob, nation, institution, group, and the individual, this group's experience illustrates the impact of mass psychology on the individual and the vicissitudes of their encounter.

REFERENCES

Amati Sas, S. (1985), Megamuertos: Unidad de medida o metáfora? *Revista de Psicoanalisis,* 42:128–137.

Amati Sas, S. (1992), Ambiguity as the route to shame. *Internat. J. Psycho-Anal.,* 73:329–334.

Amati Sas, S. & Gampel, Y. (1997), Mass sexuality, private sexuality (what sexuality, whose sexuality?). Presented at meeting of International Psychoanalytical Congress, Barcelona.

Anzieu, D. (1985), *Le Moi-Peau.* Paris: Dunod.

Berenstein, I. & Puget, J. (1997), *Lo Vincular: Clínica y Técnica Psicoanalítica.* Buenos Aires: Paidos.

Bick, E. (1968), Experiences of the skin in early object relations. *Internat. J. Psycho-Anal.,* 49:484–486.

Bick, E. (1984), Further considerations of the function of the skin in early object relations. Findings from infant observation integrated into child and adult analysis. *Brit. J. Psychother.,* 2:292–299.

Bion, W. R. (1961), *Experience in Groups.* New York: Basic Books.

Bion, W. R. (1962), *Learning from Experience.* London: Heinemann.

Bion, W. R. (1970), *Attention and Interpretation.* London: Heinemann.

Bleger, J. (1967), *Simbiosis y Ambiguedad.* Buenos Aires: Paidos.

Bowlby, J. (1973), *Attachment and Loss: Vol. 2. Separation: Anxiety and Anger.* New York: Basic Books.

Durkheim, E. (1925), *Moral Education: A Study in the Theory and Application of the Sociology of Education,* trans. E. K. Silson & H. Schnurer. New York: Free Press of Glencoe.

Falzeder, E. & Brabant, E., eds. (1996), *The Correspondence of Sigmund Freud and Sándor Ferenczi, Vol. 2, 1914–1919.* Cambridge, MA: Belknap Press of Harvard University Press.

Freud, S. (1905). *Three Essays on the Theory of Sexuality. Standard Edition,* 7:130–243. London: Hogarth Press, 1953.

Freud, S. (1915), *Instincts and Their Vicissitudes. Standard Edition,* 14:117–140. London: Hogarth Press, 1957.

Freud, S. (1919), *The Uncanny. Standard Edition,* 17:219–256. London: Hogarth Press, 1955.

Freud, S. (1920), *Beyond the Pleasure Principle. Standard Edition,* 18: 7–64. London: Hogarth Press, 1955.

Freud, S. (1921), *Group Psychology and the Analysis of the Ego. Standard Edition,* 18:69–143. London: Hogarth Press, 1955.

Gampel, Y. (1992), Psychoanalysis, ethics, and actuality. *Psychoanal. Inq.,* 12:526–550.

Gampel, Y. (1993), From the being in itself by modeling through transformation by narration in the therapeutic space. *Brit. J. Psychother.,* 19:280–290.

Gampel, Y. (1996), The interminable uncanny. In: *Psychoanalysis at the Political Border,* ed. L. Rangell & R. Moses-Hrushovski. Madison, CT: International Universities Press.

Gampel, Y. (1997), The role of social violence in psychic reality. In: *The Perverse Transference and Other Matters,* ed. J. Ahumada, J. Olagaray, A. K. Richards & J. Olagaray. Northvale, NJ: Aronson, pp. 461–470.

Gampel, Y. (1998), Einige Gedanken zu Dynamiken und Prozessen in einer Langzeitgruppe von Uberlebenden der Shoah [Some thoughts about the dynamics and process of long term large group with child and adolescent survivors of the Shoah]. *Psychoanalitische Blatter,* 9:83–104.

Gampel, Y. (1999), Between the background of safety and the background of the uncanny in the context of social violence. In: *Psychoanalysis on the Move,* ed. E. Bott Spillius. London: Routledge, pp. 59–74.

Kernberg, O. F. (1998), *Ideology, Conflict, and Leadership in Groups and Organizations.* New Haven, CT: Yale University Press.

Le Bon, G. (1895), *La Psychologie des Foules.* Paris: Félix Alcan.

McDougall, W. (1920), *The Group Mind.* Cambridge, UK: Cambridge University Press.

Moscovitz, J. J. (1998), La memoire du crime contre l'humanité. *J. Assn. Méd. Israelites de France,* 47:8–12.

Pichon-Riviere, E. (1975), *El Proceso Grupal: Del Psicoanalisis a la Psicología Social (I).* Buenos Aires: Ediciones Nueva Visión.

Puget, J. (1991), The social context: Searching for a hypothesis. *Free Associations,* 21:21–33.

Sartre, J. P. (1960), *Critique de la Raison Dialectique.* Paris: Gallimard.

Steiner, G. (1999), Errata: *Récit d'une Pensée*. Paris: Gallimard.

Wilgowicz, P. (1999), Listen psychoanalytically to the Shoah half a century on. *Internat. J. Psycho-Anal.,* 80:429.

Winnicott, D. W. (1965), The relationship of a mother to her baby at the beginning. In: *The Family and Individual Development*. London: Tavistock.

Winnicott, D. W. (1988), *Babies and Their Mothers*. London: Free Association Books.

Freud's
Group Psychology,
Psychoanalysis, and
Culture

CLÁUDIO LAKS EIZIRIK

When *Group Psychology and the Analysis of the Ego* was published, Freud was 65 years old. In the years immediately after World War I, he appeared to have a renaissance in his professional life; he was filled with hope and bursting with new ideas and plans for the worldwide diffusion of his work. During the spring of 1919, in the same wave of productivity that led him to write *Beyond the Pleasure Principle* (1920), Freud conceived the "simple idea" of an explanation of group psychology. After the usual process of taking notes and composing the first draft, his book was finished by the end of March 1921 and was published three or four months later. When he sent it as a gift to Romain Rolland, Freud, in his characteristic tone, mentioned that he did not consider *Group Psychology* particularly successful, but that it suggested a pathway from the analysis of the individual to an understanding of society.

In spite of having written it immediately after the seminal paper in which he proposed the controversial hypothesis of a death instinct, *Group Psychology and the Analysis of the Ego* had little direct connection with *Beyond the Pleasure Principle*. The ideas he developed in this book are more connected with *Totem and Taboo* (1913), *On Narcissism* (1914), and *Mourning and Melancholia* (1917). If we follow the suggestions Freud makes to the reader to look for previous papers from which his present line of thinking emerges, we will find six references to the *Three Essays*

(1905), seven to *Totem and Taboo* (1913), and three each to the papers on narcissism and mourning.

Although foreshadowed in these papers, Freud's view on mass psychology was fully developed in *Group Psychology.*

Group Psychology was first published by the Internationaler Psychoanalytischer Verlag under the title of *Massen Psychologie und Ich-Analyse.* It consists of a bold outline of the contribution of psychoanalysis to mass psychology. For the sake of uniformity, Strachey preferred to translate "masse" as "group" and justified his decision by the fact that Freud used *masse* both for Le Bon's (1895) *foule* and McDougall's (1920) *crowd.* His may be considered nowadays to be an unhappy decision; for instance, "crowd psychology" would have been more faithful to Freud's views dealing with this complex theme. For those readers like me, who, unable to follow Freud's ideas in his original German but have had the opportunity to read it in the Spanish version by Ballesteros y de Torres, who correctly called it *Psicología de las Masas,* it still produces an awkward sensation to think about the huge numbers of people to whom Freud is referring in this work as a "group."

As the title indicates concisely, *Group Psychology and the Analysis of the Ego* seeks to forge a synthesis of the two, to explain the psychology of masses on the basis of changes in the psychology of the individual mind. Additional data appear in Freud's investigation of the structure of the mind, published as *The Ego and the Id* (see Strachey, 1952; Jones, 1962; Gay, 1989; Grubrich-Simitis, 1998; Kernberg, 1998).

The relationship between ego and id, the latter not yet coined as a term within psychoanalysis, was explored at some length in the work under discussion, but it is predominantly seen as one of Freud's most interesting and brilliant contributions to understanding social processes, and it is in this light that it is considered here.

GROUP PSYCHOLOGY AND THE ANALYSIS OF THE EGO: THE BOOK

In highlighting the main ideas presented by Freud (1921), we should bear in mind that "anyone who compares the narrow dimensions of this little book with the wide extent of group psychology will at once be able to guess that only a few points chosen from the whole material are to be dealt with here" (p. 71). The same caveat applies to my intent to select out of what he modestly calls "this little book" what seems to me to constitute his main contribution to our understanding of mass psychology. As the book consists of 12 elegantly presented brief chapters, for the sake of conciseness I will devote a paragraph to each of them.

(1) In the Introduction, Freud suggests that there is not a great difference between individual and group psychology, since "in the individual's mental life someone else is invariably involved" (p. 69). With respect to social or group psychology, it is usual to isolate as the subject of interest "the influencing of an individual by a large number of people simultaneously" (p. 70). Therefore, group psychology is concerned "with the individual man as a member of a race, of a nation, of a caste, of a profession, of an institution, or as a component part of a crowd of people who have been organized in to a group at some particular time for some definite purpose" (p. 70). It might be natural to think about the phenomena that appear under these circumstances as expressions of a social instinct, a "herd instinct," or a "group mind." But it is also possible to consider that this social instinct might have its beginnings in the family.

(2) Freud moves on to the consideration that an individual changes when he becomes part of a group. How does it happen? To answer this question, Freud quotes extensively from Le Bon (1895), who described the group mind, in which the particular attributes of each individual become obliterated in the group and his distinctiveness vanishes. Le Bon suggested three new characteristics that an individual acquires as member of a group: a feeling of invincible power, derived from numerical considerations; the contagion of every sentiment and act; and suggestibility, which leads to a state of fascination similar to that observed in hypnosis. As a consequence, a group is impulsive, changeable, irritable, incapable of perseverance, omnipotent, credulous; it wants to be ruled and oppressed, fears its masters, and is entirely conservative. In brief, it is led almost exclusively by the unconscious, the group mind being identified with the mind of primitive people. The group worships the magical power of words and never thirsts after truth. A peculiar feature of the group is the "prestige" enjoyed by the leader, a sort of domination exercised by an individual, a work, or an idea.

(3) Another account of collective mental life was offered by McDougall (1920), who suggested that organization is the factor that can help in differentiating crowds from structured groups. In his view, there are five

conditions for raising collective mental life to a higher level: some degree of continuity of existence in the group; the development of an individual's emotional relation to the group as a whole; the need for interaction with other groups, perhaps in the form of rivalry; the establishment of traditions, customs and habits; and a definite structure, expressed in different functions of its constituents.

(4) What is the psychological explanation of the mental change experienced by the individual in a group? Freud, as in previous papers, once more approaching the riddle of suggestion, discusses the concept of libido and proposes that love relations constitute the essence of group mind. He suggests two arguments in favor of this proposition: 1) a group is held together by a power of some kind, and this power can only be Eros, which unites everything in the world; and 2) the individual gives up his distinctiveness and accepts the influence of other members of the group by suggestion because he needs to be in harmony with them rather in opposition to them.

(5) In the book's most creative insight into the nature of group cohesion, Freud examines two highly organized, lasting, and artificial groups, the Church and Army, and here he highlights the relation of the leader with the mass. Both Church and Army are animated by the same illusion: the leader loves all the individuals with an equal love. In the Church, this makes the believers "brothers in Christ," since before Christ, as a kind of elder brother or a substitute father, everyone is equal and everyone has an equal share in his love. In the Army, the commander is a father who loves all soldiers equally, which makes them comrades. Thus, each individual is bound by libidinal ties both to the leader and to the other members of the group. As a proof of this hypothesis, Freud mentions the outbreak of a panic after the loss of the leader in one way or another, as happened with Holofernes, whose head was cut off by Judith, leading to the dissolution of the mutual ties among the Assyrian army and to their flight from the battlefield. Considering the possible dissolution of a religious group, Freud suggests that it gives way to the appearance of cruelty, intolerance, and hostile feelings toward other people. He adds that "if differences between scientific opinions could ever attain a similar significance for groups, the same result would again be repeated with this new motivation" (p. 99).

(6) Freud turns to other problems in groups: the presence of ambivalence in all human relations, as shown in the narcissism displayed in minor

differences. But when a group is formed, whether temporarily or permanently, the natural intolerance among the individuals vanishes. Freud suggests that "love for oneself knows only one barrier—love for others, love for objects" (p. 102). He suggests that observing the state of being in love can help in understanding the libidinal ties in groups. After reiterating the main events of psychosexual development, Freud proposes that identification is the original form of an emotional tie with an object.

(7) As the original form of an emotional tie with an object, identification can become, in a regressive way, a substitute for a libidinal object-tie, by means of introjection of the object into the ego; and it may arise with any new perception of a common quality shared with someone else. The members of a group are tied by an identification of this kind. Freud suggests that the common quality lies in the nature of the link to the leader. A further step in this process is the identification with the lost object, which is introjected into the ego, something well observed in melancholia. What follows in the book is the description of a psychic agency that develops in the ego, through the introjection of the lost object. This results in the formation of the ego ideal as an agency; it comprises the moral conscience, self-observation, censorship of dreams and also serves as the main influence in repression.

(8) There are other examples of the mutual relations between the object and the ego. In the state of being in love, a great amount of narcissistic libido overflows onto the object, and we see that the latter consumes the ego, so to speak. As Freud puts it, idealization can develop to such an extent, that "everything that the object does and asks for is right and blameless"; or, to put it in a formula: "the object has been put in the place of the ego ideal (p. 113), and so the ego becomes impoverished and surrenders itself to the object. This process is different from identification, where the ego enriches itself with the properties of the object it has introjected into itself. The real question is whether the object is put in the place of the ego or of the ego ideal.

The other situation to be considered is hypnosis, where we see something similar with the exclusion of sexual satisfaction. Hypnosis, which can be seen as the situation of a group of two people, helps in the understanding of the relation of the group with the leader: "a primary group is a number of individuals who have put one and the same object in the place of their ego ideal and have consequently identified themselves with one another in their ego" (p. 116).

(9) Freud then considers and criticizes the herd instinct, a concept suggested by Trotter (1916). Freud believes that it is impossible to grasp the nature of a group without taking into account the importance of the leader. He suggests that the social feeling among the group members is based on the reversal of what was at first a hostile feeling into a positive tie in the nature of an identification. Consequently, all the members of a group are equal to one another, can identify themselves with one another, and share the desire to be ruled by one person. Freud suggests a correction to Trotter's idea that a man is a herd animal; Freud says, instead, that man is a horde animal, a group, individual creatures in a horde led by a chief.

(10) Who is this chief? Recalling Darwin's (1871) conjecture about the primal horde ruled over by a powerful male led to Freud's (1913) own hypothesis in *Totem and Taboo*. Freud now suggests that this primal father prevented his sons from satisfying their sexual impulses and forced them into an emotional tie with him and with one another. In essence, the father coerced the sons into group psychology. In the same way as the hypnotist awakens in his subject a part of his archaic heritage, "the leader of the group is still the dreaded primal father; the group still wishes to be governed by unrestricted force, it has an extreme passion for authority . . . the primal father is the group ideal, which governs the ego in the place of the ego ideal" (p. 127).

(11) After proposing that the individual gives up his ego ideal and substitutes for it the group ideal as represented by the leader, Freud discusses a differentiating grade in the ego. He explains the possibilities, presented in cases of melancholia and mania, of different conflicts between the ego and the ego ideal, the name he still employs for the superego.

(12) Many things still remain to be considered, which Freud tries to do in his Postscript. He himself has the impression, which he mentioned to Romain Rolland, of a piece of the work "not particularly successful." What *is* of particular importance is the distinction between identification of the ego with an object and replacement of the ego ideal by an object. A soldier takes his chief as his ideal, whereas he identifies with his peers. In the Church, every believer loves Christ as his ideal and feels himself united with all other believers by the tie of an identification. But he has also to identify himself with Christ and love all other believers as Christ loves them. After discussing the many dimensions of the libido theory, Freud compares the state of being in love, hypnosis, group formation, and neurosis. He states:

[B]oth states, hypnosis and group formation, are an inherited deposit from the phylogenesis of the human libido—hypnosis in the form of a predisposition, and the group, besides this, as a direct survival. The replacement of the directly sexual impulses by those that are inhibited in their aims promotes in both states a separation between the ego and the ego ideal, a separation with which a beginning has already been made in the state of being in love [p. 143].

SUBSEQUENT DEVELOPMENTS

Group Psychology and the Analysis of the Ego stimulated many studies on mass psychology and on organizational and group dynamics. A comprehensive overview of these studies and its applications to group psychotherapy, to hospital treatment and therapeutic community, to group and organizational dynamics and to leadership, culture and society can be found in Kernberg (1998). Some of these contributions are particularly relevant to the way current culture views psychoanalysis and the way psychoanalysis affects culture. For these reasons I would like to summarize some of them.

Bion (1961), one of the most creative Kleinian psychoanalysts, dealt with small (seven to twelve members) groups as an analyst sitting down with a patient. The "group-as-a-whole" exhibits a transference to the group leader in the form of a group culture, which is suffused with unspoken and unconscious assumptions shared by all the group members. The set of assumptions about the nature of the group, of its leader, of the task of the group, and of the role expected of the members has three variants, which constitute basic assumptions. The three basic assumptions are detected in the feeling tone in the atmosphere of the group.

The dependent basic assumption gives rise to a group of members, each hanging, often disappointedly, on the words of wisdom of the group leader, as if they assume that all knowledge, health, and life are located in him and are to be derived by each member individually from him.

In the fight–flight basic assumption, the members gather around the excited and violent ideal that there is an enemy to be identified and that the members will be led in a conformist phalanx by the leader against this enemy or, alternatively, in flight from it. Such an enemy may be "neurosis" itself in the therapy group, or one of the members of the group, or some suitable object outside the group (an external enemy).

The pairing basic assumption suffuses the group with a mysterious kind of hope, often with behavioral pairing between two members, or a member and the leader, as if all share the belief that some great new idea (or individual) will emerge from the intercourse of the pair (a messianic belief).

Bion contrasted the basic-assumption state of a group with what he called the "work group," in which the members address the consciously defined and accepted task of the group. In this state the group functions with secondary-process sophistication and attends to an examination of the reality inside and outside the group. The work-group state usually incorporates aspects of active basic-assumption states. Bion thought of the basic assumptions as "valences" that drew people inevitably together and established group belonging.

Bion was able to relate basic-assumption characteristics to the working of social institutions: the Army, for instance, clearly represents the fight–flight assumption. The Church may be considered as the institutional structuralization of the dependency assumption. The pairing assumption he saw in the aristocracy, an institution concerned with breeding (Hinshelwood, 1989).

Elliott Jaques (1955) described the way in which individuals may use social institutions to support their own psychic defenses. These institutional methods are collective forms of defense which Jaques called the social defense system. They come to be incorporated into the routines of the institution. Human institutions, therefore, have a subculture that is unconscious and that is highly determinant of the manner in which the institution conducts its business and the efficiency with which the individuals address their conscious tasks (Hinshelwood, 1989).

Jaques (1955) suggested that Freud's idea of the substitution of the ego ideal by an object implicitly contains the concept of projective identification, proposed by Klein (1946).

Anzieu (1971) proposed that, under conditions of regression in the unstructured group, the relationship of individuals to the group will acquire the characteristics of fusion. In his view, individual instinctual needs will be fused with a fantastic conception of the group as a primitive ego ideal, which Anzieu equated with an all-gratifying primary object, the mother of the earliest stages of development.

Chasseguet-Smirgel (1975), expanding on Anzieu's observations, suggests that under these conditions any group, small or large, tends to select leaders who represent not the paternal aspects of the prohibitive superego but a pseudopaternal "merchant of illusions." A leader of this kind provides the group with an ideology, a unifying system of ideas; in this case, the ideology is an illusion that confirms the individual's narcissistic aspirations of fusing with the group as a primitive ego ideal—the all-powerful and all-gratifying proedipal mother. In short, the small-or large-group members' identifications with one another permits them to experience a primitive narcissistic gratification of greatness and power. Violent groups operating under the influence of ideologies that have been adopted under such psychological conditions present an aggressive behavior that reflects their need to destroy any external reality that interferes with the group's illusionary ideology. In Chasseguet-Smirgel's view, the repressed ego, the id, and the primitive (preoedipal) ego ideal of each individual are fused in the group illusion.

Kernberg (1998) suggests that some of the strikingly regressive features of small groups, large groups, and mobs might be better understood in the light of our present knowledge of the internalized object relations that predate object constancy and the consolidation of the ego, superego, and id. Owing to the nature of the regression that occurs in groups, group processes pose a basic threat to members' personal identity, a threat that is linked to the tendency for primitive aggression with predominantly pregenital features to be activated in group situations. These processes, particularly the activation of primitive aggression, are dangerous to the survival of the individual in the group, as well as to any task the group needs to perform. In Kernberg's view, to follow the idealized leader of the mob blindly, as described by Freud, reconstitutes a sort of identity by identification with the leader. This identity protects the individual from intragroup aggressions by this common identity and the shared projection of aggression to external enemies and which gratifies dependency needs through submission to the leader.

There is a striking tendency in large groups, states Kernberg, to project superego functions onto the group as a whole in an effort to prevent violence and protect ego identity by means of a shared ideology. The concomitant need of all group members to project and externalize superego functions onto the leader reflects not only sadistic and idealized aspects of primitive superego precursors but also the realistic and protective aspects of more mature superego functioning.

Kernberg has also described this level of regression as characteristic of the mass psychology of conventionality; it reflects the ideology characteristic of a latency child's superego and is represented typically by mass entertainment. As an alternative, the large group evolves into a dynamic mob characterized by predominantly paranoid features, and the selection of paranoid leaders is typically represented by the mass psychology of revolutionary movements. Conventional culture, on one hand, and violent revolutionary movements with totalitarian ideology, on the other, may be considered the corresponding mass-psychological outcomes of idealization and persecution as basic group phenomena.

Reexamining Freud's essay from this perspective, Kernberg suggests that Freud's description of mass psychology corresponds chiefly to the characteristics of large groups and to mob and horde formation. Freud's emphasis on the libidinal links among members as a defense against envious rivalry corresponds precisely to the condensation of and defense against the preoedipal, and particularly oral, envy and oedipal rivalry that characterize the activation of primitive object relations during large-group processes.

Reaching beyond the restricted psychoanalytic community, *Group Psychology and the Analysis of the Ego* has had an impressive, even fundamental, impact on philosophers, particularly the Frankfurt school; on sociologists, particularly Mitscherlich in Germany, Moscovici in France, and Lasch in the United States; and possibly on another of the great 20th-century humanists, Elias Canetti (Kernberg, 1998).

All these developments represent only a small part of the enormous amount of work produced in the 80 years since the publication of *Group Psychology and the Analysis of the Ego*. They are a testimony of the ongoing influence of Freud's book.

Let us turn now to another area, the challenging field of the relationship between psychoanalysis and culture, and try to find out whether Freud's ideas can help us to understand this complex situation.

PSYCHOANALYSIS AND CULTURE: FRIENDS OR FOES?

The account of the complex relationship between psychoanalysis and culture begins in the city of its birth. Psychoanalysis was born in fin-de-siècle Vienna, a cultural milieu in which the "intelligentsia" was developing innovations in many areas simultaneously (Eizirik, 1997). The

Viennese cultural elite had a rare combination of provincialism and cosmopolitanism, tradition and modernism, which produced a sort of cohesion greater than in other cities. The Viennese cafés and the frequent cultural meetings were solid institutions that kept their vitality as places and moments when intellectuals communicated ideas and values, thus stimulating each other (Schorske, 1980). Recently, Renato Mezan (1996) explored the contrasting views on this relationship held by Bruno Bettelheim and Peter Gay. Bettelheim (1991) considered that Viennese culture revealed the curious simultaneity of the Empire disintegration and the apex of intellectual development, in which the understanding of ambivalence, hysteria, and neurosis was a natural consequence; in other words, psychoanalysis could not have appeared in any place but Vienna. In contrast, Peter Gay (1989) believes that psychoanalysis could perfectly well have developed elsewhere, a point of view also endorsed by Mezan (1996).

Whether we accept Gay's and Mezan's view or we hold to the one suggested by Bettelheim, there will probably be no dispute as to the enormous influence of psychoanalysis on Western culture in the subsequent decades, "when all intellectuals were playing with the ideas of Freud and his followers" (Sanville, 1996, p. 15). Its enormous influence was widespread, with varying impacts in different places. But the shared excitement and interest that the new field of knowledge raised existed almost everywhere. This general trend, with regional differences, was well documented by Peter Kutter (1992–1995).

More recently, however, "the humanistic culture concerned with the development and maturation of the individual, with self-exploration and subjectivity is being questioned by a cultural trend to immediate adaptation and social effectiveness, that has led to a decrease in the interest in psychoanalysis on the part of cultural and intellectual elites" (Kernberg, 1996, p. 39).

In spite of the many problems (scarcity of patients, criticisms from different areas, challenges to psychoanalysis as an effective method of treatment, and so on) that led to the general designation of an "actual crisis of psychoanalysis" (Cesio et al., 1996), "in many university settings psychoanalytic thinking has continued to grow, for example in the area of literary analysis, art, and the humanities in general" (Kernberg, 1998, p. 40).

A recent example of the ambivalent attitude toward psychoanalysis can be found in Harold Bloom's (1994) *The Western Canon,* in which he explores the Western literary tradition by concentrating on the works of 26 authors central to the Canon, among whom he includes Freud. Bloom considers his "possibly the best mind of our century" (p. 373) or "a powerful and sophisticated mind . . . indeed it is the mind of our age" (p. 375). In his view, however, Freud was subject to a literary influence and its anxieties; in this sense, Shakespeare was the real inventor of psychoanalysis, and Freud, only its codifier. Bloom goes so far as to say that "Shakespeare is everywhere in Freud, far more present when unmentioned than when he is cited" (p. 391) and that "Freud was anxious about Shakespeare because he had learned anxiety from him, as he had learned ambivalence and narcissism and schism in the self" (p. 394). Bloom's attitude is deliberately provocative: he concedes that psychoanalytic thinking has deeply penetrated into Western culture, but, at the same time, and, in part, because of that influence, he wishes to diminish Freud's originality.

Perhaps the best-known recent flash point for the expression of the current cultural ambivalence toward psychoanalysis was the postponement, in 1996, of the Library of Congress exhibition on Sigmund Freud, said to be due to a lack of funding. The delay, provoked in the first instance by a petition of a group of scholars who felt that the planned exhibition was too one-sided and asked for balance, rapidly burgeoned into a murky if often heated debate. But many of the supporters of the exhibition believed that at least some of the petitioners were proposing that Freud was irrelevant to current thought. The point to be made here is that the delay, whatever its cause, demonstrated some tension in the current relationship of psychoanalysis to the culture. The exhibition, entitled "Sigmund Freud: Conflict and Culture," was finally held in Washington, in 1998, and then in other cities of the United States, Latin America, and Europe. One of its products is the outstanding and balanced book edited by its curator (Roth, 1998).

In previous work (Eizirik, 1997), I suggested that psychoanalysis is currently facing four main challenges in the culture: (1) the changing nature of the philosophical and cultural cross-currents of contemporary Western culture as they influence psychoanalysis as a discipline; (2) the challenge of the empiricist's scientific tradition to the hermeneutic approach in psychoanalysis; (3) attacks on psychoanalysis as an elitist discipline and profession; and (4) the movement away from subjectivist and existential concerns to a focus on a collectivist and pragmatic relation to reality.

How can our knowledge of group psychology help us to widen our understanding of these current challenges?

DISCUSSION

Is it possible to imagine the psychoanalytic movement as an artificially structured group, as the Church or the Army described by Freud? If we do so, it is not difficult to suppose that the first period after the "splendid isolation" was characterized by a great idealization of psychoanalysis, of its explanatory power (Eizirik, 1998), of its therapeutic effectiveness, and of its almost omnipotent and omniscient creator, "indeed the mind of our age" (Bloom, 1994, p. 375).

In spite of some doubts and criticism, the prevailing view was full of hope and high expectations. Freud and his new discipline can be seen as the object in which a thousand ego ideals were vested. Freud was, in a sense, the Commander-in-Chief. The Psychoanalytic Army fought many battles and conquered, one after the other, cities, universities departments of psychiatry, but mainly many thousands of minds. Partly owing to the effectiveness of many analytic therapies, partly owing to the excitement that led intellectuals to play with Freud's ideas (Sanville, 1996), and partly owing to the magical expectations it raised, this period can also be viewed as embodying the basic assumption of dependency described by Bion (1961).

Even after Freud's death, the powerful ideas he left behind him continued to act as the necessary ego ideal. Even after he was dead, Freud did not cease to be the psychoanalysts' ego ideal. In each of the societies and study groups established in the three regions where the IPA exists (Kutter, 1992–1995), it is possible to identify one or two main leaders who, acting as Freud did, became the ego ideals of their own communities. But after the early years, as we know, members of the psychoanalytic movement did not display among themselves the kind of love that Freud believed was present in the Army or even in the Church. To combat dissension, two successful mechanisms were employed, first by Freud and then by his followers: the projection of the conflicts toward external enemies to defend "the cause" and the reinforcement of idealization of the leader or of the discipline itself. From time to time, someone was sacrificed and expelled, carrying with him or her the evil or bad objects (for example, Jung, Adler, and Heimann) as in a fight–flight basic assumption.

If we now consider the second and present state of affairs, what do we see? Psychoanalysis is under attack from many sides and subject to growing criticism. A disturbing question has been raised: how relevant is psychoanalysis to our culture at present? (Person, 1997, personal communication). As a result of this "malaise," similar to that of an army that has lost its commander-in-chief, similar to that of a Church that cannot introject and find comfort in the magical words of its God or Christ, parts or large sections of the psychoanalytic community fight each other or flee to other groups, perhaps those that are more reassuring, for example, biological psychiatry. One issue currently demanding research is the cause of the enormous amount of energy expended in many endless disputes within psychoanalysis (Eizirik, 1997).

I suggest that at the center of this puzzling question is exactly what Freud taught us in *Group Psychology*. He clearly spoke of an illusion. And we believed in this illusion for the first 50 or 60 years: the illusion of omnipotence, omniscience and shared love. Now we blame Freud for offering us this illusion. And a good way of blaming him is to behave like a leaderless Army or a Church without faith. We could go further with this analogy by saying that Christ later on was betrayed, denied, and sacrificed. In a sense, something similar may be under way with regard to Freud and his ideas, as a result of the bitter disillusionment produced by the current challenges we are facing. This bitterness is expressed in two apparently opposite ways. On one hand, many analysts adopt the dogmatic position that Freud is the only thinker to be studied and considered; and, on the other hand, some analysts reject the value of Freud's ideas to our current theory and practice and replace them by one or another author or school, which in turn becomes the idealized source of all knowledge. It is not difficult to understand that in the kernel of both positions there is an attack produced by the frustration of the former illusion.

As Kernberg (1998) suggests, we may possibly be witnessing, to some extent, the regressive phenomena presented by large and small groups, whose morality is influenced by projection of primitive superego functions. As Kernberg puts it, "Freud's description of the ambivalent relation to leadership—the combination of idealization and what might be called paranoid fears of the leader with submission and subservience to him—reflect the struggle between idealizing and persecutory processes that is characteristic of large groups and mobs" (p. 43). The leader—Freud, psychoanalysis—thus represented a reassurance against inner conflicts or, in Jaques's (1955) terms, constituted a social system that protected all the members of this community against schizoparanoid and depressive anxieties.

In spite of the huge conscious effort to keep psychoanalysis alive and well, both as a discipline and as an institution, I think we must recognize that this ambivalent relation with Freud and his seminal ideas is currently a worldwide phenomenon in the psychoanalytic community. A possible symptom of it is the frequently observed ambivalence toward the IPA, the institution established by Freud to develop and protect psychoanalysis during its necessary growing process. Rivalry, competition, envy, narcissism, false dichotomies (research versus clinical activity), dogmatic positions (causing the painful and long process required to obtain official acceptance of concentrated analysis), all might be seen as other symptoms of this ambivalence.

At the same time, in spite of the recurrent reports on the crisis, isn't there something weird in the very fact that psychoanalysis remains alive and growing each year, and its many publications continue to appear, and its meetings continue to attract people, and the much criticized IPA remains one of the most solid and respected international scientific institutions?

Isn't it interesting to hear from a visitor to the Freud Exhibit, not a psychoanalyst, that in spite of considering that "the degree (if any) to which Freud's theories are applicable to psychiatric treatment today is a key point for discussion . . . very few practitioners of psychiatry or psychology . . . will deny the existence of the unconscious (which has now been captured by functional brain imaging), that patients develop a transference to the doctor or therapist, or that those in turn develop a countertransference to the patient?" (Licinio, 1998, p. 2198). What has all this to do with the complex relation between psychoanalysis and culture? In my view, a great deal.

We should take into account that psychoanalysis is a product of modernity. As François Lyotard (1991) has pointed out, "modern societies based their discourses on truth, justice and in the great historical and scientific meta-narratives. The present-day crisis is precisely the crisis of these discourses" (p. 11). In contrast to modernity, the postmodern condition privileges skepticism, recognizes the complexity of the world (which leads to a weakening of such concepts as progress or absorption of the old into the new), challenges the simplistic notion of power (all power is relational, there are pockets or "micropowers " in each system), accepts the right of being different and the social demands for participation (citizenship and rights of women, pacifists, homosexuals) (see Arditi, 1988).

If we consider the current complexity and the openness required of all theories, we may also question the somehow simplistic model offered by Freud in his description of group psychology. Even if we consider the further contributions presented by his followers, we must still feel that such accounts are fragmentary and incomplete, privileging exclusively the psychological side and almost ignoring biological, social, economic, and anthropological factors. After all, we may think in dismay, Freud's description might be another illusion. And this is, in my view, the main idea he put forward: the idea of an illusion. "Everything depends upon this illusion; if it were to be dropped, then both Church and army would dissolve" (p. 94).

This said, what I have in mind is that the illusory power of psychoanalysis is over. Of course, it still exists in our consulting rooms, in the analytic relationship that allows us to obtain our remarkable therapeutic results through the artificial construct of the transference neurosis and its resolution. But as a theory, as a discipline, and as an institution, psychoanalysis now requires verification of theories, outcome studies, and a permanent dialogue with other disciplines.

In the present-day, postmodern mental set, illusions are no longer welcome, nor is reliance on past authority. The pursuit of a whole and unifying theory, the view of psychoanalysis as a metanarrative, with strong explanatory power, is part of that illusion. The same holds true for the illusion of a training system of worldwide application that does not take into account the cultural and historical factors of each region. And the same can be said of the idea of psychoanalysis as the only treatment and not just one form of psychotherapy.

Complexity, fragmentation, skepticism, the right to be different, growing social demands—in a way, aren't these the elements of the present state of psychoanalysis as a training system, as a treatment, as an institution, as a group of different theories sheltered under the same umbrella?

At the beginning of a new millennium and of our second century we are now challenged to give up our illusions, to demonstrate to our surrounding culture that we answered its thirst for illusion with the partial belief in some illusions but that we are now part of a structured, predominantly work group whose members are tied together with the same purpose of undoing illusions, our own and the prevailing ones in our culture.

Yes, Professor Freud, the struggle is not yet over.

REFERENCES

Anzieu, D. (1971), L'illusion groupal. *Nouv. Rev. Psychanal.,* 4:73–93.

Arditi, B. (1988), La posmodernidad como coreografia de la complejidad. XVIII Congreso Latinoamericano de Sociologia, Montevideo.

Bettelheim, B. (1991), *A Viena de Freud e Outros Ensaios*. Rio de Janeiro: Campus.

Bion, W. R. (1961), *Experiences in Groups*. New York: Basic Books.

Bloom, H. (1994), *The Western Canon*. New York: Harcourt Brace.

Cesio, F., Eizirik, C. L., Ayala, J., Sanville, J., Casas de Pereda, M. & Israel, P. (1996), *The Actual Crisis of Psycho-Analysis: Challenges and Perspectives*. Report of the House of Delegates Committee on the Crisis of Psychoanalysis. London: IPA.

Chasseguet-Smirgel, J. (1975), *L'Idéal du Moi*. Paris: Claude Tchou.

Darwin, C. (1871), *The Descent of Man*. Princeton, NJ: Princeton University Press, 1996.

Eizirik, C. L. (1997), Psychoanalysis and culture: Some contemporary challenges. *Internat. J. Psycho-Anal.,* 78:789–800.

Eizirik, C. L. (1998), Alguns limites da psicanálise: Flexibilidades possíveis. *Rev. Bras. Psicanál.,* 32:953–965.

Freud, S. (1905). *Three Essays on the Theory of Sexuality. Standard Edition,* 7:130–243. London: Hogarth Press, 1953.

Freud, S. (1913). *Totem and Taboo. Standard Edition,* 13:1–162. London: Hogarth Press, 1953.

Freud, S. (1914a), *On Narcissism: An Introduction. Standard Edition,* 14:69–102. London: Hogarth Press, 1957.

Freud, S. (1914b), *On the History of the Psychoanalytic Movement. Standard Edition,* 14:3–66. London: Hogarth Press, 1957.

Freud, S. (1917), *Mourning and Melancholia. Standard Edition,* 14: 243–258. London: Hogarth Press, 1957.

Freud, S. (1920), *Beyond the Pleasure Principle. Standard Edition,* 18: 3–64. London: Hogarth Press, 1955.

Freud, S. (1921), *Group Psychology and the Analysis of the Ego. Standard Edition,* 18:65–143. London: Hogarth Press, 1955.

Gay, P. (1989), *Freud: Uma Vida Para o Nosso Tempo.* São Paulo: Companhia das Letras.

Grubrich-Simitis, I. (1998), Nothing about the totem meal: On Freud's notes. In: *Freud: Conflict and Culture,* ed. M. Roth. New York: Knopf.

Hinshelwood, R. (1989), *A Dictionary of Kleinian Thought.* London: Free Association Books.

Jaques, E. (1955), Social system as a defense against persecutory and depressive anxiety. In: *New Directions in Psycho-Analysis,* ed. M. Klein, P. Heimann & R. Money-Kyrle. New York: Basic Books, pp. 478–498.

Jones, E. (1962), *Vida y Obra de Sigmund Freud.* Buenos Aires: Editorial Nova.

Kernberg, O. (1996), Letter of the House of Delegates. In: *The Actual Crisis of Psycho-Analysis: Challenges and Perspectives,* ed. F. Cesio, C. L. Eizirik, J. Ayala, J. Sanville, M. Casas de Pereda & P. Israel. Report of the House of Delegates Committee on the Crisis of Psychoanalysis. London: IPA, pp. 37–41.

Kernberg, O. (1998), *Ideology, Conflict and Leadership in Groups and Organizations.* New Haven, CT: Yale University Press.

Klein, M. (1946), Notes on some schizoid mechanisms. In: *Developments in Psychoanalysis,* ed. J. Rivière. London: Hogarth Press, 1952, pp. 292–320.

Kutter, P. (1992–1995), *Psychoanalysis International: A Guide to Psychoanalysis Throughout the World, Vols. 1–3.* Hillsdale, NJ: The Analytic Press.

Le Bon, G. (1895), *La Psychologie des Foules.* Paris: Félix Alcan.

Licinio, J. (1998), Expressing Freudian influences. *Science,* 282:2197–2198.

Lyotard, J. F. (1991), Interview. *Zona Erogena.*

McDougall, W. (1920), *The Group Mind.* Cambridge, UK: Cambridge University Press.

Mezan, R. (1996), Viena e as Origens da Psicanálise. In: *A Formação Cultural de Freud,* ed. M. Perestrello. Rio de Janeiro: Imago.

Roth, M., ed. (1998), *Freud: Conflict and Culture.* New York: Knopf.

Sanville, J. (1996), The crisis. Concept evidences and possible responses. In: *The Actual Crisis of Psycho-Analysis: Challenges and Perspectives,* ed. F. Cesio, C. L. Eizirik, J. Ayala, J. Sanville, M. Casas de Pereda & P. Israel. Report of the House of Delegates Committee on the Crisis of Psychoanalysis. London: IPA, pp. 12–19.

Schorske, C. (1980), *Fin-de-Siècle Vienna.* London: Weidenfeld & Nicolson.

Strachey, J. (1962), Editor's note. In: Freud, S. (1921), *Group Psychology and the Analysis of the Ego. Standard Edition,* 18:65–143. London: Hogarth Press, 1955.

Trotter, W. (1916), *Instincts of the Herd in Peace and War.* London: Unwin.

Contributors

DIDIER ANZIEU was co-editor of the first paleographic edition of the *Pensées of Pascal*. Gravitating toward psychoanalysis from 1949 he took part in the foundation of the Psychoanalytical Association of France (APF) in 1963. Professor of Psychology in the Faculty of Arts at Nanterre, Member of the APF, he published many works on psychoanalytic theory. He was a longtime member of the IPA and a major contributor to the psychoanalytic literature.

ROBERT CAPER is a training and supervising analyst at the Psychoanalytic Center of California, Assistant Clinical Professor at the UCLA School of Medicine, a member of the Editorial Board of the *International Journal of Psychoanalysis,* and author of two books: *Immaterial Facts: Freud's Discovery of Psychic Reality and Klein's Development of His Work,* and *A Mind of One's Own.*

CLÁUDIO LAKS EIZIRIK is a training and supervising analyst of the Porto Alegre Psychoanalytical Society, Adjunct Professor in the Department of Psychiatry of the Federal University of Rio Grande do Sul, and Chair of the Program of MsC and PhD in Psychiatry. He is President of FEPAL, chair of the IPA Committee on Psychoanalysis and Society, and IPA Associate Secretary for Latin America.

ERNST FALZEDER is a clinical psychologist and historian of psychoanalysis, one of the editors of the Freud–Ferenczi correspondence, and author of many publications about the history of psychoanalysis. He was supported by the Louis Jeantet Award for research in the history of medicine (Geneva, Switzerland), is a fellow of the Smithsonian Institute in Washington DC, and is a guest professor at Harvard.

YOLANDA GAMPEL is a Professor in the Psychology Department and Psychotherapeutic Program of the School of Medicine, Tel Aviv University. She is a Training Analyst of the Psychoanalytical Society of Israel and of the International Psychoanalytical Association.

ANDRÉ E. HAYNAL is a supervising and training analyst and former President of the Swiss Psychoanalytic Society (IPA), an honorary member of the Hungarian Psychoanalytic Society, Professor of Psychiatry (emeritus and honorary) at the University of Geneva (Switzerland), and former visiting professor at Stanford University (U.S.). In addition to his other works, he is co-author of *Fanaticism: A Historical and Psychoanalytic Study*.

JOHN KERR is Senior Editor at The Analytic Press. A writer, clinical psychologist, and historian, he is a member of the Section on the History of Psychiatry, New York University/Cornell Medical Center, author of *A Most Dangerous Method: The Story of Freud, Jung, and Sabina Spielrein*, and co-editor of *Attachment Theory: Social, Developmental, and Clinical Perspectives*.

ETHEL SPECTOR PERSON is Professor of Clinical Psychiatry, Department of Psychiatry, College of Physicians and Surgeons, Columbia University; Training and Supervising Analyst at the Columbia Psychoanalytic Center for Training and Research, and a member of the American Psychoanalytic Association. She is Chair of the IPA Committee on Publication and has previously served as Associate Secretary and Vice-President of the IPA for North America. Among her books are *Dreams of Love and Fateful Encounters* and *The Sexual Century*.

ABRAHAM ZALEZNIK is the Konosuke Matsushita Professor of Leadership (Emeritus), Graduate School of Business Administration at Harvard University, certified in Psychoanalysis and an active member, American Psychoanalytic Association. In addition to being a major business consultant, he has written widely about organizational issues.

Index

Abraham, K., 4, 42
  analysands, 126
Acton, J., 99
adhesive identification, 139
aggression, xxii, 49–50, 58, 163. *See also* violence
  stirring up and disinhibition of, 9, 58
alienation, 134–135
Amati Sas, S., 132, 133
analyst(s)
  "family trees" of early analysands and, 124–128
  as "real" vs. phantasy object, 71–75
analytic dyad
  as pairing group, 84–85
  as primitive *vs.* sophisticated group, 69–70
    clinical illustration, 72–76
  as Specialized Work Group, 78–84
analytic relationship(s)
  as "real" *vs.* transference relationship, 71–75
  types of, 83
Anzieu, D., 57, 137, 138, 162
Arditi, B., 170
Army, 13, 17–18, 24, 49, 78, 87, 167
aspiration, 64–66
authoritarian analysis, 82
authority, 90, 97, 105–108
  importance, 95–96, 100
  legitimacy, 100

need for direction, obedience, and, xvi–xvii
  power and, 92, 94
authority figures. *See also* leader(s)
  variability in behavior of, 97–98
autonomy, ego
  relinquishment of, 89
Ayala, J., 165

Barrows, S., 46
basic assumption groups, 76, 78, 81–82, 135. *See also* pairing group; primitive group
basic assumptions, 54–55, 67–68, 77, 79, 83, 135, 161–162
Becker, E., xvi–xvii
Berenstein, I., 136
Bettelheim, B., 165
Bick, E., 137, 139
Bion, W. R., 53–55, 67–68, 78, 84, 135, 137, 138, 161, 167
Bleger, J., 135
Bloom, H., 165–167
boards of directors, 93
Bolterauer, L., 116
Bowlby, J., 137
Brabant, E., 4, 130

Canetti, E., xiii–xvi
Caper, R., 64n, 73n, 74, 78
Casas de Pereda, M., 165